Financing from Masses

Jiazhuo G. Wang · Hongwei Xu
Jun Ma · Yexia Zhang · Zhi Chen
Editors

Financing from Masses

Crowdfunding in China

Springer

Editors
Jiazhuo G. Wang
College of Staten Island
City University of New York
Staten Island, NY
USA

Hongwei Xu
Shanghai Wenxi Investment Consulting Co.
Hongkou District, Shanghai
China

Jun Ma
Shanghai Wenxi Investment Consulting Co.
Hongkou District, Shanghai
China

Yexia Zhang
Shanghai Wenxi Investment Consulting Co.
Hongkou District, Shanghai
China

Zhi Chen
Shanghai Wenxi Investment Consulting Co.
Hongkou District, Shanghai
China

ISBN 978-981-10-5842-4 ISBN 978-981-10-5843-1 (eBook)
https://doi.org/10.1007/978-981-10-5843-1

Library of Congress Control Number: 2017948202

Printed on acid-free paper

This Springer imprint is published by Springer Nature
The registered company is Springer Nature Singapore Pte Ltd.
The registered company address is: 152 Beach Road, #21-01/04 Gateway East, Singapore 189721, Singapore

Preface

As a new volume in the book series on China's Internet finance and small business financing, it seems to be an appropriate time now to discuss and analyze another remarkable financial innovation in China in the recent years, which is the well-publicized crowdfunding. In fact, I personally touched this subject well before I scholastically studied it, and even now, I can still remember my first time to see a physical and real-life crowdfunded project in China a few years ago. It was a summer weekend in Shenzhen, a city located next to Hong Kong and widely perceived as the Silicon Valley of China, when and where I was invited to give lectures at the HSBC Business School of Peking University (PKU) as a visiting professor. On that sunny Saturday afternoon, one of my PKU alumni took me to join a seminar at a PKU club called Wei Ming Café (or Unnamed Café in Chinese, following the name of the famous Wei Ming Lake in PKU's Beijing campus), which was crowdfunded by 200 PKU alumni with RMB 50,000 from each individual. The café is well sited on the top of a high rise, overseeing the Shenzhen River and Hong Kong on another side of water, and all the investors of the café are entitled to use this facility for their various activities as part of their return package as a shareholder of this crowdfunded property. I was truly impressed by the design, decoration, and view of the club; however, as a professor of finance, I was more excited to personally see a real and concrete example of crowdfunding in China for the first time.

Similar to other financial innovations such as online lending, the primary functionality of crowdfunding is to provide an online platform, through which both the party that seeks financing and the party that is able and willing to supply funds can interface with each other in order to transfer the funds from the hands of the investors (or the surplus economic units) to the hands of fund recipients (or the deficit economic units) at previously agreed-upon terms. As the business model of the crowdfunding enables the demand side and supply side of a funding process to interact directly and cuts out the intermediary functions that were previously provided by many financial institutions, crowdfunding could considerably simplify the funding and investment process and significantly reduce the financing cost for the project initiators that seek funding for their start-ups and/or innovative projects in terms of either money or time.

Unlike these earlier Internet-based innovations, such as online lending or online payment, however, crowdfunding is a relatively late comer in China and possibly involves the transfer of equity ownership of the funded projects, instead of only funds transfer as did by debt financing. By its very nature, debt type of financing, including online lending, may not be an ideal way of financing for these start-ups and innovative projects at early stages, as (1) the start-ups and innovative projects at early stages are, typically, still in their phase of "burning money" with heavy focus on research and development, without immediate cash inflows. As a result, it could be difficult for these start-ups to timely fulfill their obligations to pay the periodical interest incurred by the debt financing; (2) both start-ups and innovative projects are facing tremendous uncertainty and risk, and in some sense, their success is pretty much a matter of probability. It is truly not uncommon for observing many early-stage investments to fail badly due to various reasons. As a result, repayment of the fund principal to fund lender at the maturity may become a "mission impossible" for the unsuccessful start-ups and the innovative project initiators if the projects are funded by debt financing; (3) the fund providers of debt financing are typically the investors with lower tolerance for risk taking, which is, likely, the primary reason for why they did not invest in the equity securities that typically provided higher returns but with higher risk. As a result, using the funds from the relatively conservative investors to finance the highly risky projects may bring tremendous risk that could be "unexpected" or "unbearable" by these conservative investors and may not be "morally" justified, either. Therefore, as an approach involved in equity stakes, crowdfunding paved a new alternative path of financing for small business, in general, and start-ups, in particular.

The value of crowdfunding for project initiators, investors, and crowdfunding platform operators, at the micro-level, could be very profound. For the project initiators, especially for these start-ups with relatively smaller size in financing needs, and the projects with relatively less "significance" in value comparing with these projects with "breakingthrough" innovations in technologies, it is usually difficult for them to obtain equity financing at such early stage of their growth cycle. Even the financial innovations such as the development of angels and venture capitals may not be adequate to address the financing issues of these start-ups, as the cost of information collection, risks inherited in these projects, and the possible returns that these projects are expected to provide for these early-stage investors may not be well justified for a positive decision. As a result, many "valuable" but less "significant" innovations may not be able to even get a chance to be "born," not mentioning to grow and flourish, even though they are, indeed, an indispensable and integrated component of advance in technologies and progress of society.

For the online platform operators, the rise of crowdfunding represents a strategic and timely opportunity for their transition and business development. Many online platforms in China emerged with the growth of P2P online lending in an unregulated market environment in the first decade of the century. As an innovative way to integrate Internet and finance and targeting the uncovered and underfinanced groups in the society, such as micro- and small businesses, borrowers with smaller fund needs, and consumers with lower income, the fast growth of P2P online lending in the past years went far beyond the expectation of almost everyone in the market. As the core component of the online lending process, the growth of platforms also reached its peak during the same period of time. However, as the risks inherited in the online lending got more exposed over time and the fraud incidents appeared more frequently in the headlines of media, the hummer of the regulators eventually came down. Meanwhile, with the increased regulations is the entry of the capital from "mainstream," such as state-owned enterprises, commercial banks, and listed companies, with the resources that the "grassroots" platforms are difficult to compete with.[1] As a result, exit from online lending industry and identifying the new outlet became a critical issue for these existing online platform operators, and crowdfunding provided a timely option for them.

From investment perspective, crowdfunding also provides small- and medium-sized investors in China with an alternative investment opportunity in a financial environment where the stock market has been bearish for years, real estate risk has been rising, and commercial banks' deposit rates have had significant difficulty catching up with rising inflation rates. Some investment opportunities with relatively higher returns, such as portfolio investment provided by some wealth management services or entrusted investment by some commercial banks, all set up relatively high thresholds for participation which disqualified many investors with relatively smaller idle money to invest, and the development of crowdfunding provided a niche opportunity for this specific segment of the investor groups. As a result, crowdfunding not only can satisfy the equity financing needs of SMEs and start-ups, it also more effectively utilizes the idle funds in the economy, improves the efficiency of fund usage, and enhances the basic functionality of the financial market in transferring surplus funds from the holder of the surplus funds to demander of the funds. Essentially, like other financial innovations, crowdfunding helps improve the efficiency of resource allocation in financial market.

At the macrolevel, the development of crowdfunding may help China's transformation from an economy primarily driven by low-labor-cost, investment, and export to an economy primarily driven by innovation and domestic consumption, when Chinese economy is at a crossroad. In the past years, the passage of Labor Law[2] and increased income and standard of living in China have made the cost of labor no longer be an advantage for the competitiveness of "Made in China" products, as evidenced by sharply increased overseas investment and relocation of many manufacturing facilities from China to various less developed countries, such as Vietnam, India, and Cambodia, and even to some developed countries, such USA and western European countries. On the other hand, the sluggish economic recovery and growth worldwide and overcapacity of production in China also made

[1]Wang, J.G. and Xu, H., Co-edited, 2015, Financing the Underfinanced—Online Lending in China, Springer.

[2]http://www.gov.cn/banshi/2005-05/25/content_905.htm.

both export and domestic investment hard to continue to play the driving engine role for Chinese economic growth in the next decades, even though the "Belt and Road Initiative"[3] proposed by Chinese leaders in the recent years attempts to explore a new outlet for China's products and production capacity, especially in the areas of infrastructure. As a result, an innovation-driven and domestic-consumption-oriented growth strategy will become vital for China's sustainable economic growth for the next decades, and small- and medium-sized enterprises (SMEs) and their massive innovations are expected to play a critical role under this new strategy.

Historically, the role played by SMEs in China's economy was considered somewhat insignificant. Under the traditional ownership structure, the majority of SMEs are privately owned firms that were either set up as a private one since their inceptions or transferred from state-owned during the period of time of ownership reform in 1990s. Compared to large state-owned corporations and their roles as the dominant force in the economy, SMEs were typically perceived as relatively trivial entities whose primary functionality is to fill market niches and cover the few segments uncovered by large state-owned corporations. As a result, SMEs and the financing of SMEs were not perceived as a top priority issue on the agenda of China's economic development in the past.

However, that page of the China's economic growth has been turned over, and the role of SMEs, and especially their innovations, in economic growth has been much better understood and recognized by entrepreneurs, scholars, policy makers, and general public in recent years in China. The plain fact that the progress in economic growth is simply and persistently the result of "creative destruction," as Joseph Schumpeter pointed out several decades ago,[4] now became well-known common knowledge in China. Innovation from the marketplace internally drives the growth of the economy, while entrepreneurs are the initiators and executors of such innovations. Innovation-driven growth, along with the participation of entrepreneurs and millions of SMEs, will be the key to breaking the vicious cycle.

The participation of SMEs in innovation is certainly important for improvement in economic inclusiveness. However, their impact can go far beyond that. SMEs not only make up the majority of the total number of firms in an economy, and can conduct innovations in many areas that larger corporations cannot cover, but they also have stronger motivation to innovate in the first place. By nature, innovations —especially the fundamental ones—are changes or destructions in existing product and market structure, and the larger firms typically benefit more from the status quo. As a result, large corporations, usually, may tend to be less motivated to innovate than SMEs. Kodak, for example, was widely considered a classic case of a large corporation in a monopolistic position, who resisted new digital technology innovation due to a conflict of interest with its traditional film business, and eventually

[3]http://baike.baidu.com/item/%E4%B8%80%E5%B8%A6%E4%B8%80%E8%B7%AF/13132427.

[4]Schumpeter, J., 2006, Capitalism, Socialism and Democracy, New Edition, Routledge, London.

filed for bankruptcy. Therefore, SMEs are widely expected to play a much more critical and strategic role, instead of a niche one as before, in China's sustainable economic growth in the coming decades.

However, despite the new tasks that SMEs have been expected by the market to undertake, obtaining adequate funding to support innovation and entrepreneurship has been a difficulty for many such small and medium companies. In a monetary economy, conducting innovation without funding would be like driving a car without gasoline or electricity. The difficulties in financing SMEs under the traditional financial system in China remain a huge hurdle that companies must overcome before the Chinese economy can emerge from a non-sustainable growth model to a sustainable one. As a result, financial innovations, including crowdfunding, would be a necessary condition for a successful economic transition in China. In addition to indirect financing with traditional bank loans and focus on the large amount of funding as provided by large state-owned commercial banks, infrastructure for direct financing and funding for smaller amount of financing request, especially equity financing, also needs to be in place. The emergence and development of crowdfunding is simply a timely and tailored response to the ever increased demands for China's growth model transformation, in general, and financing for SMEs and start-ups, in particular.

Another significance of the fast development of crowdfunding in China could be the tremendous opportunities it may bring to the business community worldwide, especially global investors. As the economy with large, and in many occasions the largest, number of cell phone owners, Internet subscribers, online shoppers, online social media participants, undercovered fund demanders, and overliquid fund suppliers, Internet-related industries could become one of the pillar industries in China in the next decades, just like the auto industry in the USA in the last century. Some early comers, such as Yahoo from USA and Softbank from Japan, have sweetly tasted the harvested fruit from their venture capital investment in Alibaba, an award for their visions and insights. It can be expected that the crowdfunding, like online lending, that grew from grass roots may trigger a sequence of the shake-up of China's financial industry, accelerate the integration of Internet and finance, and bring in enormous investment opportunity for the business community worldwide.

However, like all other financial tools that facilitate business transactions, crowdfunding also holds potential risks that the financed projects may fail to achieve what was expected and are unable to provide the financial and non-financial returns that were anticipated by investors, and there also exists a trade-off between risks and returns. In particular, as a way of equity financing, crowdfunding does not promise the return of the investment principal back to the investors, as debt financing did, and the risk inherited in crowdfunding could be even higher than that of online lending. Crowdfunding shattered the monopolies of large financial institutions in financing channels, but cannot nonetheless eliminate the uncertainties inherent to investment itself, such as the information asymmetry between the parties of transactions and uncertainty in the future. In fact, because of the involvement of the Internet and the lack of adequate due diligence as usually conducted by traditional financial institutions, the crowdfunding and other online business models may exacerbate even higher level of asymmetry and, consequently, the risk. Just as the inappropriate use of financial derivatives, which were originally created to prevent and reduce risks, ended up in the largest financial crisis since World War II, crowdfunding, while it may stimulate financial innovation, may introduce new risks due to it being an Internet-enabled financing solution.

It is therefore imperative to conduct a comprehensive analysis of this burgeoning industry to explore the value that crowdfunding will provide for start-ups, project initiators, platform operators, investors, and businesses while simultaneously identifying root causes of the potential risks of this financial innovation and suggest possible solutions for mitigating these risks. From this perspective, "Financing from Masses—Crowdfunding in China" could be a timely publication that may be valuable for a wide spectrum of readerships.

This book covers the most important areas and issues in the crowdfunding industry in China, including, but not limited to, the definition of crowdfunding, the history of crowdfunding, the scale of the crowdfunding market, the basic business models and a risk analysis of crowdfunding, market analysis of some sub-industries of crowdfunding, some case studies of several mainstream crowdfunding platforms, government regulations and policies related to crowdfunding, financing of crowdfunding platforms, and finally, the outlook for crowdfunding industry in the future. As a book that combines theoretical analysis and real-world practices in China's crowdfunding industry, it could be of interest and value to a variety of readers, including, but not limited to, the following.

First, institutional and individual investors both inside and outside China may find this topic relevant and intriguing. Financial institutions such as security firms, investment banks, private equity funds, venture capital firms, commercial banks, other financial intermediaries, and individual investors including angels could gain a better understanding about the crowdfunding industry in China. In particular, SME and start-up financing involves many smaller-amount financial transactions, which will provide investment opportunities for smaller investors who may not be able to participate under the traditional financial regime.

Second, Chinese SMEs and start-ups with innovative projects that are looking for financing should also be interested in this topic. As China adapts its growth model into a more innovation-oriented one, obtaining adequate equity funding becomes a critical prerequisite for success. Understanding what is available, and which method of financing can best meet SMEs' needs and match the nature of their business, would be of tremendous value for SMEs and start-ups that are operating in China. For example, debt financing may better fit the working capital needs, while equity financing may be more appropriate for R&D and start-ups.

Third, investors and professionals who are running alternative financial entities, such as online crowdfunding platforms, may also take an interest in this topic. Like the running of any other financial operation, running an alternative financing entity not only provides an innovative business opportunity for the parties that are engaged, but also exposes the alternative financial operators to the new risks associated predominantly with these new financial services. As a result, they would have an urgent need to supplement their knowledge and understanding about this changing industry, especially its risks and the potential downfalls, in order to maximize their bottom line returns and mitigate risk. Therefore, this book will indubitably be an important reference tool for them.

Fourth, bankers in traditional financial institutions such as commercial banks might be interested in this book as well. New alternative ways of financing, especially Internet-related innovations such as crowdfunding, can be reasonably considered as both a formidable challenge and a lucrative opportunity for traditional financial institutions. Opening the door for private equity and the integration of finance and Internet has been recognized as both an indomitable and irresistible trend, and the "anywhere, anytime, anyway, and customer experience" has become fundamental to all service industries, including finance. As this trend grows at an increasingly high pace, the critical question facing the traditional commercial banking system is how traditional banks can promptly meet this challenge, and in a more competitive market environment besides, as evidenced by the newly established joint ventures between these China's largest commercial banks [Industrial and Commerce Bank of China (ICBC), Agricultural Bank of China (ABC), and China Construction Bank (CCB)] and China's Internet giants (JD, Baidu, and Alibaba).[5] Gaining thorough understanding of the status quo of the current financial market and new alternative financial innovations will become a prioritized item for traditional commercial bankers and their major shareholders, domestic and international. This book would certainly provide an important reference for that purpose.

Fifth, members of regulatory agencies could find value in this book as well. In China, the financial industry is strictly regulated, and any new "innovations" will be closely "watched" by regulatory agencies. Even though more explicit legislation regarding certain new alternative financing methods, such as crowdfunding, has not been fully delineated yet, it is merely a matter of time before regulatory agencies bring the hammer down; this is true especially because the general public has become increasingly exposed to the risks associated with new alternative methods as the public gains more knowledge and understanding about these "innovations." The major dilemma in government regulation, however, is always the extent or degree to which regulations should be set up and implemented. While overregulation can unnecessarily hinder the innovations needed for business development and economic growth, under-regulation may fail to control the risks that will damage said business development and economic growth. As a result, a comprehensive analysis and understanding about the new alternative financing such as crowdfunding is a prerequisite for the regulators, in order to help them achieve the optimal balance between regulation and market innovation. This book could offer some valuable insights.

Sixth, academics inside and outside China could be interested in this book as well. Because the growth model of the Chinese economy has fundamentally changed, and even more changes are expected down the road, the role of SMEs in

[5]http://news.hexun.com/2017-06-23/189755761.html.

Chinese economic growth in the next decades has been redefined, and SMEs' status has been repositioned. Understanding how SMEs can be financially funded so that they can survive and succeed is a key to understanding the new growth model of the Chinese economy. Any research on the China's future economic growth omitting the topic of SMEs and their relationship with financial innovation would be incomplete. In this regard, this book would provide such Chinese business researchers with a valuable reference.

In summary, as China increasingly becomes a key player in the world economy, understanding the dynamics in Chinese economy, in general, and the innovations in financial market, in particular, becomes increasingly critical. As the impact of the recent "Belt and Road Forum"[6] indicated, the influence of the Chinese economy on the global one cannot be underestimated. Therefore, we hope this book "Financing from Masses—Crowdfunding in China" will be a well-timed publication with important value for a wide spectrum of readerships, either as a reference book or as a guideline in understanding, gaining knowledge of, research and teaching, and making business decisions about China's financial market.

New York, USA Jiazhuo G. Wang

[6]http://www.beltandroadforum.org/.

Acknowledgements

This book is a result of a joint effort of the researchers from City University of New York, the Small and Medium Enterprises Research Center of the HSBC Business School at Peking University, Online Lending House (WangDaiZhiJia), and Yingcan Consultation (Yingcanzixun). The book is co-edited by Dr. J. George Wang and Hongwei Xu, and the associate editors are Jun Ma, Yexia Zhang, and Zhi Chen.

For the writing of the book, Dr. J. George Wang wrote the preface, and the original chapters were written in Chinese. Among them, Yexia Zhang, Zhi Chen, and Haimei Wang wrote Chap. 1; Zhi Chen, Haimei Wang, and Xingqiang Yuan wrote Chap. 2; Zhi Chen and Haimei Wang wrote Chaps. 3, 4, and 7; Zhi Chen wrote Chap. 5; Zhi Chen, Haimei Wang, and Lixiu Gao wrote Chap. 6; and Yexia Zhang and Zhi Chen wrote Chap. 8. Dr. J. George Wang, Jun Ma, Yexia Zhang, and Baichen Yu reviewed and revised all above chapters in Chinese, and Dr. J. George Wang rewrote the entire book in English and finalized the book for its submission.

In addition, Allison Wang of the Stern School of Business at New York University edited and proofread the book. Wei Zhao and Hannah Qiu of Springer Publisher provided much support along with the production of this book. All the efforts and contributions of the above individuals toward the publication of this book are greatly appreciated. Of course, the authors are solely responsible for any errors and omissions.

Contents

Chapter 1
An Overview of Crowdfunding in China

Yexia Zhang, Zhi Chen and Haimei Wang

1.1 The Definition, Origin and Classification of Crowdfunding

1.1.1 The Definition of Crowdfunding

Crowdfunding can be generally defined as a practice of funding a project or venture by raising monetary contributions from a large number of people,[1] or the use of small amounts of capital from a large number of individuals to finance a new business venture through social media and crowdfunding websites with the potential to increase entrepreneurship by expanding the pool of investors beyond the traditional circle of owners, relatives and venture capitalists.[2] There are primarily three types of participants in crowdfunding: fundraisers, platform operators and investors. Among them, fundraisers are project initiators who create projects on crowdfunding platforms, introduce their products, creativity or needs to the market, and set up financing window period, financing models, financing amount and expected returns. Platform operators are crowdfunding website owners/managers that are responsible for examination and display of the projects that are created and submitted by fundraisers, and providing service support. Finally, investors are the individuals who select appropriate projects for their investment through crowdfunding platforms.

Similar definitions about crowdfunding were also provided by some international organizations, such as International Organization of Securities Commissions, and government agencies, such as People's Bank of China.

[1]https://en.wikipedia.org/wiki/Crowdfunding.
[2]http://www.investopedia.com/terms/c/crowdfunding.asp.

Y. Zhang (✉) · Z. Chen · H. Wang
Shanghai Wenxi Investment Consulting Co., Shanghai, China
e-mail: zhangyx@wdzj.com

J.G. Wang et al. (eds.), *Financing from Masses*,
https://doi.org/10.1007/978-981-10-5843-1_1

According to International Organization of Securities Commissions, crowdfunding refers generally to obtaining funds of small amount from many individuals or institutions via online platforms, which are used to provide funds for a certain project, business or personal loans and other needs.[3] Crowdfunding is also included by the People's Bank of China in The China Financial Stability Report (2014) as one of the six main businesses of China's internet finance, and defined as the model of small amount funding for projects or business activities that were initiated by sponsors via network with certain returns to investors.[4]

Compared with traditional ways of financing, crowdfunding provides wider open access for both start-up entrepreneurs and investors to the projects with smaller-amount of monetary value, and the financial benefit of the involved projects is no longer taken as the only consideration for funding. Any project could be financed with the initial funds through crowdfunding as long as it is well received by fund suppliers. The smaller scale of initial funding also provides tremendous opportunities for smaller-sized investors to participate.

1.1.2 The Origin of Crowdfunding

The origin of crowdfunding can actually be traced back to 18th century. A British poet Alexander Pope planned to translate a 15,693-line ancient Greek poetry Homer into English in 1713, asking each subscriber to pledge two gold Guineas (an old British currency) to support his work. In return, Pope promised to include an acknowledgment of everyone who pledged. This creative commitment brought in more than 500 supporters, and more than 4000 Guineas were raised to help him complete the translation work.[5]

With the fast development and wider applications of the internet in recent years, a much more effective and efficient way of crowdfunding—internet-platform-based crowdfunding surfaces. Since 2007, a large number of crowdfunding platforms have emerged in Europe and the United States. In April 2009, the world's largest and most influential crowdfunding platform—Kickstarter went online officially, which began to help entrepreneurs successfully raise funds right after its establishment,[6] and quickly drew wide attention of the entire society. As a public recognition of this totally new financing method, the word "crowdfunding" was formally included in Macmillan Dictionary and Oxford Dictionary, in February 2010 and November 2011, respectively.[7]

---

[3]https://www.iosco.org/.

[4]http://rmb.xinhua08.com/a/20140429/1320967.shtml.

[5]https://en.wikipedia.org/wiki/Alexander_Pope; http://shareproperty.co.uk/a-history-of-crowdfunding/.

[6]https://www.kickstarter.com/.

[7]http://www.macmillandictionary.com; https://www.oxforddictionaries.com/.

Table 1.1 History of development of crowdfunding industry in China

2011	The first domestic crowdfunding platform Demohour went online, which marked the inception of China's crowdfunding industry
2013	Taobao crowdfunding, a subsidiary of Alibaba, went online officially, which indicated the entry of the e-business giants into crowdfunding industry
2014	The number of crowdfunding platforms in China reached 100
2015	Other China's internet giants, such as JD, Tencent, Suning, Baidu, Qihoo 360 and Letv began to step into the crowdfunding industry
2016	The subindustries of crowdfunding, such as used cars, physical stores, film and television, and other cultural products, developed rapidly; the total number of platforms surpassed 400, and the total amount of funds that were successfully raised reached RMB 20 billion

Data Source www.yingcanzixun.com

In China, the first crowdfunding platform, Demohour, which supported the industry of hardware with artificial intelligence, emerged in 2011.[8] As a low-threshold, well-diversified and highly innovative way of financing, crowdfunding greatly improves the effectiveness of funding of start-ups, and provides an alternative channel for smaller investors with idle resources. With the encouragement of Chinese government policy of "Massive Entrepreneurship and Innovation",[9] a great number of crowdfunding platforms and innovative projects have been developed since its inception. Table 1.1 shows the chronicle of the crowdfunding industry in China.

1.1.3 The Classification of Crowdfunding

Crowdfunding can be divided into four categories: Rewards-based crowdfunding, Equity-based crowdfunding, Charity-based crowdfunding, and Debt-based crowdfunding.

1. Rewards-based crowdfunding is a type of fundraising by a company with tangible products, services, or certain rights and benefits as a return to the investors. The varying level of awards are typically set up according to the pledged funding amount, which is usually less than $100,000. Rewards crowdfunding is also the most popular option for crowdfunding in China at present, which involves the industries of smart hardware, agriculture, used cars, and film and television, with various return forms. Project initiators issue the product information through the platforms, and investors who have interest may choose to

[8]www.demohour.com/.

[9]http://www.gov.cn/zhengce/content/2015-06/16/content_9855.htm.

purchase or finance the posted project. Apparently, rewards-based crowdfunding can also perform the functionality of the traditional market research to certain degree, and help the project initiators obtain the information of demands for their forthcoming products directly and effectively.

2. Equity-based crowdfunding is a way of financing through the exchange of actual shares of a private company for capital from investors. With equity crowdfunding, project initiators can set up investors' caps and minimum pledge amounts, which is typically $100,000 or more, and approve or deny the request of the investors who wish to view the business documents of the target firms. Under equity crowdfunding, investors and project initiators will jointly undertake the risks and share the benefits as well. In China, Securities Association of China once announced that the term of "private equity crowdfunding" in Paragraph (10) of Article 2 of "Management of Filing of Over-the-Counter Securities" is modified to include "internet-based non-public equity financing", following the "Notice on Conducting Special Examination of the Financial Institutions with Equity Financing Activities via Internet" issued by China Securities Regulatory Commission (CSRC).[10] Therefore, "non-public equity financing" and "equity crowdfunding" will be used exchangeably in this book.
3. Charity-based crowdfunding, as the name stated, is the fundraising for social causes and charities without requirement of anything with value in return. The required pledge amount is usually less than $10,000. The launching of the charity crowdfunding projects follow the specific rules of different crowdfunding platforms, and its difference with traditional charity financing lies in its low threshold and massive participation.
4. Debt-based or lending-based crowdfunding allows project initiators to raise funds in the form of loans that they will pay back the principals to the lenders over a pre-specified period of time with a pre-determined interest rate. The lending-based crowdfunding well fits the financing needs of the project initiators who are not willing to give up immediately the equity in their startups, and P2P online lending belongs to lending-based crowdfunding. The investors can invest in financing projects listed on P2P online lending platforms with pre-determined interest as return, and receive their principals at maturity. This book does not contain the discussion of lending-based crowdfunding, and the interested readers can read "Financing the Underfinanced—Online Lending in China" for more detailed discussions.[11]

[10]http://www.csrc.gov.cn/pub/newsite/zjhxwfb/xwdd/201508/t20150807_282509.html.

[11]Wang, J.G. and Xu, H. Eds, 2015, Financing the Underfinanced—Online Lending in China, Springer.

1.2 The Nature and Characteristics of Crowdfunding

As an innovative way of funding start-ups and micro-businesses, crowdfunding could provide timely and critical financial resources for these innovation-oriented projects and enterprises for their birth and growth at their infancy times, and, of course, it can help broaden the financing channels for large corporations as well. Importantly, crowdfunding could allow the companies with financing difficulties to focus on their core business activities, such as design, production and services, marketing, and sales, instead of raising the needed funds in a financial market that typically favors more for the existing and well-established entities.

In addition, crowdfunding would also allow the fundraising firms to test water in the market for their forthcoming new products or services before they actually start the production and operations, which could help reduce the probability of failure of the projects in a significant way, and increase the rate of survival and success of the innovative start-ups. For the welcomed projects or products, the fundraising firms can also use the marketing information collected through financing process as an important reference for the pricing of their forthcoming new products or services.

Another important feature of crowdfunding lies in its ability to integrate various types of resources that are needed for the success of the start-ups. Under the model of crowdfunding, such as rewards crowdfunding, many investors of the fundraising firms are also the customers of the these firms, and a financing activity can also perform a functionality of cultivating loyal users, primary users, and seed users for the fundraising firms. Meanwhile, what the investors may bring into the start-ups may not only be limited to the funds that are certainly needed by the firms, but also many other valuable resources such as business connections that the start-ups may not possess, management and operating experience that the new firms typically lack, and deeper understanding about the market and future development of the industry that can only be shared by some seasoned industrial veterans. As all these resources will play an indispensable role in the growth of the start-ups, crowdfunding is truly a desirable way to integrate all the critical resources together to support the development of the innovative projects and enterprises.

Compared with traditional way of financing, another distinct feature of crowdfunding is its low threshold of the investment, which will allow a large number of smaller investors to participate, and collect funds in a much faster way with the high efficiency of the internet. An important implication of the low threshold and large number of participation is the lowered risk for each individual investor by this much more widely diversified way of investment, which, in turn, will help further speed up the growth of this emerging market.

Furthermore, crowdfunding manifests the development trend of "disintermediation" of the financial industry since the emergence of the internet finance. By allowing the related parties of the transactions to meet with each other directly through the internet platforms of the crowdfunding companies, the financing and investment process can be completed without the involvement of the traditional "intermediation", such as investment banks, private equity funds, and other financial institutions, which will significantly reduce the cost of financing and improve the efficiency of resources allocation in the financial market.

In summary, the crowdfunding may possess the following distinct features:

1. Low threshold for both project initiators and investors: At present, there is no restrictions for the qualifications of the project initiators. Any projects can be submitted to the crowdfunding platforms for review and listing, and the platform will assess the projects based on the value of the projects, instead of the credentials of the project initiators. Similarly, there is no restrictions for the qualifications of the investors, either. While crowdfunding, as an equity investment if it is an equity crowdfunding type, may bring higher risk for non-professional investors, the lowed threshold and massive participation can help reduce or offset in large part of the risk of equity investment.
2. Diversified project contents: Crowdfunding can be applied not only to various projects, but also different types of components of the projects. In addition to the functionality and technology that were usually supported by traditional financing, the crowdfunding can also support the innovations on the parts of the products in terms of packaging, music, drawing, and photography.
3. As a marketing and sales tool for a financing process: As many investors of the crowdfunding, especially in the case of rewards crowdfunding, are also the buyers or consumers of the products, crowdfunding can also serve as the process of marketing research and water test for the new products. The information collected from this financing process can be helpful from marketing and sales perspective as well.
4. An effective platform for integration: It is nothing new for an investor to bring to the fundraising firm more than just funding. The investor could provide the fundraising firms with the management skill, business connections, market resources, and better understanding about the industry and its future development, as did by many traditional investment bankers, private equity fund managers, and other seasoned financial professionals. What is new for the crowdfunding platforms lies in its much larger scale of participation of the various types of investors, who may bring in more types of non-monetary resources and higher efficiency for the completion of the entire financing process due to the use of internet. As a result, crowdfunding appears as a more effective way for resources integration.
5. Similar to other financial innovations through internet, such as P2P online lending, crowdfunding represents another step of "disintermediation" taken by the financial industry in the field of equity financing. While, as any innovations, it may bring in new risk for the financial transactions, crowdfunding certainly helps simplify the financing process and improve the efficiency of resource allocation for the financial market.

1.3 The Major Events of Crowdfunding Industry in China: 2015 to September 2016

- Guidelines on Development of Internet Finance Issued

On July 18, 2015, the People's Bank of China issued the Guidelines on Healthy Development of Internet Finance,[12] which defined the equity crowdfunding as, primarily, an activity of small-amount equity financing via internet, and requested the equity crowdfunding to be conducted through the internet platforms, such as web sites or similar electronic medias, of the financial intermediaries. Within the restrictions of the current laws and regulations, the equity crowdfunding intermediaries are allowed to explore and develop new business models, and make the equity crowdfunding an integrated part of multi-level financial market in China to better serve the financing needs of innovation and entrepreneurship.

- Stricter Regulations on Crowdfunding

On August 7, 2015, China Security Regulatory Commission (CSRC) issued the Notice on Special Examinations of Equity Financing Activities via the Internet (hereinafter referred to as the Notice in this paragraph),[13] and the CSRC Notice to Local Governments for Regulations of Equity Financing Activities via Internet,[14] aiming to rectify the online equity financing activities in China. According to the requirements of the Notice, some equity crowdfunding activities, by nature, are the non-public equity financing or private equity fundraising via the internet. As a result, these activities must follow the regulations on non-public equity financing or private equity fundraising, which means that, without the approval of the equity financing regulators of the State Council, any institutions or individuals are not allowed to conduct any equity financing activities under the name of equity crowdfunding.

- The First Law Suit on Equity Crowdfunding Ruled

On September 15, 2015, the first lawsuit in the equity crowdfunding industry in China was ruled in Beijing's Haidian District Court.[15] The judge decreed that the plaintiff, Fit Network Technology Co., Ltd. (or Ren Ren Crowdfunding Platform), wins the lawsuit, and the defendant, Nuomiduo Catering Management Co., Ltd., needs to pay the plaintiff the entrusted financing fees RMB 25,200 and penalty RMB 15,000, but Fit Network Technology Co., Ltd. needs to return the contributed (crowdfunded) capital RMB 167,200 to Nuomiduo Catering Management Co., Ltd. at the same time.

---

[12]http://www.gov.cn/xinwen/2015-07/18/content_2899360.htm.

[13]http://www.gov.cn/xinwen/2015-08/07/content_2909930.htm.

[14]http://www.csrc.gov.cn/pub/newsite/zjhxwfb/xwdd/201508/t20150807_282509.html.

[15]http://tech.sina.com.cn/i/2015-12-23/doc-ifxmttcq1856529.shtml.

- Pilot Projects of Equity Crowdfunding Launched by CSRC

On December 25, 2015, "The Opinions on Implementation of Further Improvement of the Direct Financing Ratio to Optimize the Financial Structure"[16] was announced by CSRS at a Policy Briefing of China's State Council, which included the equity crowdfunding as one of the five key priorities of development of China's financial market in 2016. At the briefing, Fang Xinghai, Vice Chairman of CSRC specified that the equity crowdfunding pilot project will start in 2016.

- Entry of Internet Giants into the Field of Equity Financing

In 2016, several non-public equity financing platforms were set up by some Internet giants, such as Qihoo 360 (360 Taojin), Suning (Suning Private Equity), Baidu (Baidu Baizhong), and Xiaomi (Micfunding), on January 5, April 6, April 18, and September 26, 2016, respectively.[17] So far, all China's internet giants including Alibaba, Baidu, JD, Qihoo 360 and Xiaomi have become the players of equity crowdfunding.

- Forthcoming Regulations on Equity Crowdfunding Announced by State Council

On February 4, 2016, "The Opinions of the State Council on Further Preventing and Disposing Illegal Financing"[18] was officially issued. The Opinions require the acceleration of the regulations on private financing and new forms of financing, issuance of the rules for the organizations involved in non-deposit-type of loan transactions, regulations on the entity of private financing market, and expansion of legal financing channels. Meanwhile, the regulators planned to issue the regulatory rules on P2P online lending and equity crowdfunding as soon as possible, to promote the development of internet finance in a way that is in compliance with the regulations, conduct research on the policies related with the wealth management of private financing intermediaries and non-financing type of guarantees, and timely issue the policies that support business and financial system reforms.

- The Charity Law Promulgated

On March 16, 2016, the National People's Congress Standing Committee held its fourth plenary meeting in Beijing. The Charity Law was passed and formally implemented from September 1, 2016. The Article 31 of the Charity Law specifies that any organization or individual without the permission or license for public fundraising shall not be allowed to publicly raise funds, but are permitted to work with charity organizations with such permission to conduct public fundraising, and the raised funds should be managed by the charity organizations with the permission for public fundraising.

---

[16]http://www.gov.cn/zhengce/2015-12/24/content_5027324.htm.

[17]www.yingcanzixun.com; http://www.wdzj.com/news/baogao/30753.html.

[18]The Opinions of the State Council on Further Preventing and Disposing Illegal Financing. The State Council of China, 2015, No. 59.

- Real Estate Crowdfunding Prohibited in Shenzhen and Guangzhou

On March 18, 2016 and April 12, 2016, Shenzhen Internet Finance Association issued the Notice on Prohibiting "Crowdfunding Speculation" in Real Estate Industry and the Notice on Stopping Real Estate Crowdfunding, respectively. On April 21, 2016, following Shenzhen's actions, Guangzhou Association of Financial Industry, Guangzhou Internet Finance Association and Guangzhou Real Estate Brokerage Association jointly issued the Notice on Stopping Down Payment Loan and Purchasing Real Estate Property by Crowdfunding, closing the way of purchasing the real estate property using down payment loan and crowdfunding.[19]

- The Establishment of National Internet Finance Association of China

On March 25, 2016, the Conference on the Establishment of National Internet Finance Association of China (NIFAC) and its first Member Representatives' Meeting was held in Shanghai. On June 22, 2016, the setup of the National Internet Finance Association of China was approved by the China's Ministry of Civil Affairs,[20] which indicated that the first national Internet Finance Association in China now came into being. The official website and the WeChat public APP of National Internet Finance Association of China went online formally on September 8, 2016. The web site contains the Association Profile, Association Dynamics, Policies and Laws, Industry Standards, Industry Disciplines, Association Members, Investor Educations, and other sections, but the functions of Association Member Inquires is not opened yet at present.

- One-Year Rectification of Internet Finance Industry Implemented by State Council

On April 14, 2016, fourteen ministries and commissions of the State Council jointly held a meeting via TV, and announced a one-year long special rectification in internet finance industry in China. On the same day, the State Council approved and released all the implementation documents covering 7 programs.[21] The involved government agencies include the Central Bank, China Banking Regulatory Commission (CBRC), CSRC and China Insurance Regulatory Commission (CIRC) (or One Bank and Three Commissions), which will be responsible to issue special rectification rules in the fields of online payment, peer-to-peer lending, equity crowdfunding, and Internet insurance.

- Regulating Equity Crowdfunding via the Amended Securities Law

On April 27, 2016, at a symposium that were jointly organized by multiple State Council agencies focusing on preventing and disposing illegal fundraising, CSRC expressed its intention to issue rules on regulating private fundraising, officially

---

[19] http://finance.sina.com.cn/roll/2016-04-12/doc-ifxrckae7839350.shtml.

[20] China Economic Weekly: http://finance.sina.com.cn/roll/2016-03-25/doc-ifxqssxu8182790.shtml.

[21] Guangming Daily: http://www.gov.cn/xinwen/2016-04/22/content_5066718.htm.

define the equity crowdfunding through amendment of Securities Law, and guide financial innovation activities to be developed in a way in compliance with the enhanced regulations. The key point was to prevent illegal financial activities from abusing the name of financial innovation.[22]

- New Third Board Listing Denied

On May 27, 2016, National Small-and-Medium Enterprise Share Transfer System issued "The Notice on Listing and Financing of Financial Enterprises.[23] The Notice divided financial enterprises into three categories: financial enterprises that are regulated by "One Bank and Three Commissions", private fundraising institutions, and other enterprises with the financial natures, and specified that the listing applications of these "other financial enterprises" are not accepted temporarily before the relevant regulations are released. For the applying enterprises that don't belong to the financial enterprises but have more than 20% (including 20%) of shares of any financial enterprises or are the largest shareholders of such firms, their applications will not be accepted temporarily, either. For already accepted applications, the review process shall be terminated.

- Signals from Lujiazui Financial Forum

On June 12–13, 2016, Lujiazui Forum, jointly sponsored by Shanghai Municipal Government, the People's Bank of China, CBRC, CSRC and CIRC, was held in Shanghai.[24] The theme of the forum was "Financial Reform and Challenge of Global Economic Growth". Jiang Yang, vice chairman of CSRC, emphasized at the meeting the importance of regulating internet equity financing activities and preventing the risks in the private fundraising and equity crowdfunding.

- The First Crowdfunded Movie Released

On July 3, 2016, the cartoon Big Fish and Begonia, which attracted much attentions of netizens, was showed in Chengdu.[25] The list of thousands of financial sponsors via crowdfunding appeared at the end of the movie and surprised all audiences. In 2013, Big Fish and Begonia launched the crowdfunding plan in Demohour, which, eventually, received supports from more than 3500 investors with funding of RMB 1,580,000. Liang Xuan and Zhang Chun, the co-directors of the movie, acknowledged that it is the crowdfunding that made this movie possible.

[22]Netease Finance: http://money.163.com/16/0428/08/BLNNNT6K00251LDV.html.

[23]National Small-and-Medium Enterprise Share Transfer System: Notice on Listing and Financing of Financial Enterprises. Announcement of the Share Transfer System (2016), No. 36.

[24]Online Lending House: http://www.wdzj.com/news/guandian/29811.html.

[25]Online Lending House: Crowdfunding Monthly Report, http://www.wdzj.com/news/baogao/31260.html.

- Equity Crowdfunding Pilot Program Issued by Guangdong Government

On July 4, 2016, Guangdong Provincial Government issued "The Notice on Further Supporting Immigrant Workers to Start Business in Hometowns",[26] which intended to strengthen the financial support for immigrant workers to start a business when they went back to their hometowns, by using Guangdong Entrepreneurial Seed Funds and engaging social capitals. In the areas where the start-ups showed great potentials, equity crowdfunding should be experimented to expand the scale of direct financing.

- The Acquisition of First Crowdfunding Platform Demohour

On July 27, 2016, Xu Zewei, the CEO of 91 Finance confirmed that Demohour has been acquired by 91 Finance, and it will be operated independently in the future.[27] Demohour will keep its current name after acquisition, and become a module of 91 Finance focusing on the crowdfunding of cultural creativity businesses.

- Thirteen Charity Crowdfunding Platforms Recognized

On August 22, 2016, China's Ministry of Civil Affairs released its recognition of the first group of 13 Charity Fundraising Information Platforms in China from a formal review of 29 candidates.[28] By the ranking score from high to low, these 13 platforms include: Tencent Charity, Taobao Net, Ant Financial Group, Sina-Weibo (Micro Charity), Fun in Funding, China Charity Information Platform, JD Charity, China Foundation Center Net, Baidu Charity Platform, Gongyibao, Xinhua Charity Service Platform, United, and Guangzhou Charity Information Platform.

- P2P Online Lending Platforms Banned on Equity Crowdfunding Business

On August 24, 2016, CBRC, together with China's Ministry of Industry and Information, Ministry of Public Security, and the State Internet Information Office, jointly published "The Provisional Measures for Management of Business Activities of P2P Online Lending Information Intermediaries".[29] The Measures prohibited P2P online lending information intermediaries from conducing any asset securitization business, and disallowed these intermediaries to be engaged in 13 business activities including equity crowdfunding.

[26]http://www.gdhrss.gov.cn/publicfiles/business/htmlfiles/gdhrss/s60/201610/58736.html.

[27]http://finance.caijing.com.cn/20160729/4155798.shtml.

[28]http://www.mca.gov.cn/article/zwgk/tzl/201608/20160800001529.shtml.

[29]CBRC: Provisional Measures for Management of Business Activities of P2P Online Lending Information Intermediaries, CBRC (2016), No. 1.

- The State Council Opinions on Venture Capital Investment Issued

On September 20, 2016, the State Council issued "Opinions on Promoting the Sustainable and Healthy Development of Venture Capital Investment".[30] which well recognized the roles played by venture capital investment in expanding the investment and financing channels of enterprises, endorsing economic structural changes and industrial transformation, increasing the ratio of direct financing in the corporate capital structure, encouraging the private fund financing of the real sectors, and stimulating entrepreneurial innovation and employment growth. In addition, the Opinion also encouraged all venture capital activities including angel investments, standardization of the development of internet-based equity financing platforms, and information and technical services for all types of entrepreneurship and innovations.

[30]The State Council: Opinions on Promoting the Sustainable and Healthy Development of Venture Capital Investment, State Council (2016), No. 53.

Chapter 2
Statistic Analysis of China's Crowdfunding Industry

Zhi Chen, Haimei Wang and Xingqiang Yuan

2.1 The General Status of Crowdfunding Platforms

2.1.1 The Number and Distribution of Platforms

By the end of September 2016, there were 415 crowdfunding platforms with normal operations in China, which was 100 platforms more comparing with the number at the end of 2015. According to the first three quarters' data in 2016, the total number of the platforms grew steadily, and it is expected that, by the end of 2016, the number of crowdfunding platforms in China with normal operations could exceed 450 (Fig. 2.1).

2.1.2 The Registered Capital of Platforms

By the end of September 2016, among the 415 crowdfunding platforms with normal operations, 42% of them filed with the Industrial and Commercial Administration with the registered capital between RMB 10 million and RMB 50 million, followed by the group of platforms with the registered capital between RMB 1 million and RMB 5 million (19%); the number of the platforms with the registered capital between RMB 5 million and RMB 10 million is accounted for about 17%; and the platforms with the registered capital between RMB 50 million and RMB 100 million and those with the registered capital more than RMB 100 million are accounted for 11% and 8%, respectively; and finally, the platforms with the registered capital less than RMB 1 million are only accounted for 3%.

Z. Chen (✉) · H. Wang · X. Yuan
Shanghai Wenxi Investment Consulting Co., Shanghai, China
e-mail: chenzhi@wdzj.com

J.G. Wang et al. (eds.), *Financing from Masses*,
https://doi.org/10.1007/978-981-10-5843-1_2

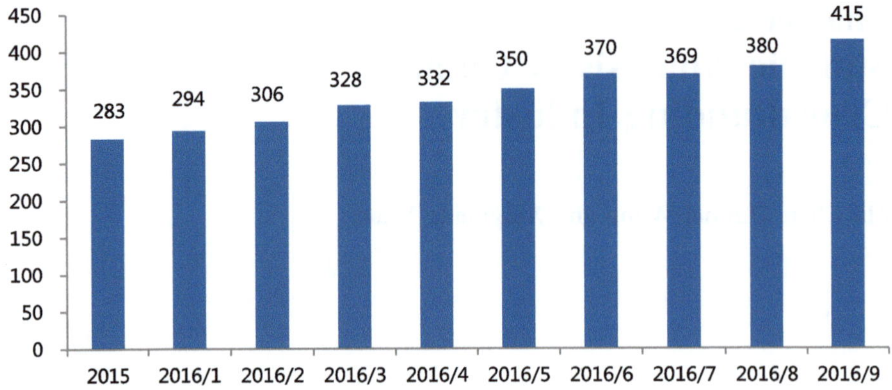

Fig. 2.1 Number of crowdfunding platforms in China with normal operations. *Data Source* www.yingcanzixun.com

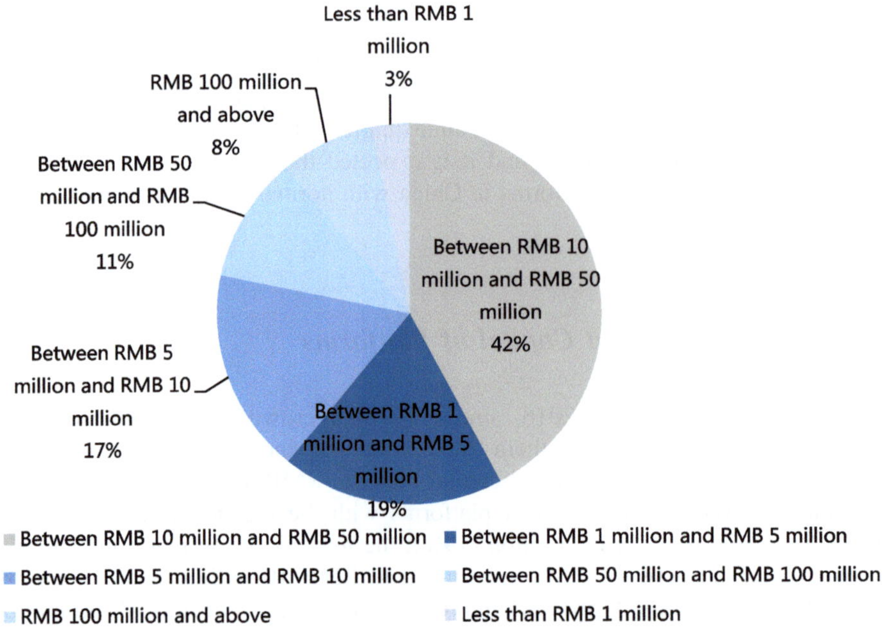

Fig. 2.2 Distribution of registered capital of platforms with normal operation. *Data Source* www.yingcanzixun.com

At present, the average registered capital of crowdfunding platforms is more than RMB 1 million, while most platforms have a registered capital between RMB 5 million and RMB 50 million, and only a few ones with the registered capital less than RMB 1 million (Fig. 2.2).

2.1.3 *The Amount of Funds Successfully Raised by Platforms*

In 2015, the crowdfunding industry in China raised RMB 11.424 billion in total, which broke the mark of RMB 10 billion for the first time in history, and was 5 times more than the amount of funds raised in 2014. From January 2016 to September 2016, the crowdfunding industry in China raised RMB 11.801 billion in total, which exceeded the total amount of funds raised in the whole year of 2015. It was expected that, by the end of 2016, the amount of funds successfully raised in the entire 2016 will exceed RMB 15 billion (Fig. 2.3).

2.2 Some Analysis of the Development of Crowdfunding Platforms

2.2.1 *The Types of Crowdfunding Platforms*

By the end of September 2016, among the 415 crowdfunding platforms with normal operations, there were 207 reward crowdfunding platforms, increasing by 213.64% compared with year end number of 2015; there were 131 equity crowdfunding or non-public equity financing platforms, which was pretty much same as the number at the year end of 2015; the number of charity crowdfunding platforms increased by 62.5% compared with 2015; and the number of mixed-type (containing more than one type) crowdfunding platforms decreased by 13.92%, compared with 2015 (Fig. 2.4).

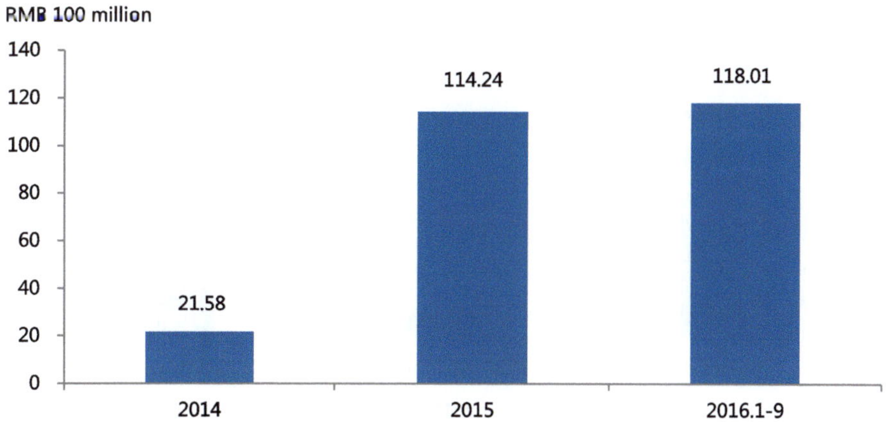

Fig. 2.3 The amount of funds raised by crowdfunding industry in China over the years. *Data Source* www.yingcanzixun.com

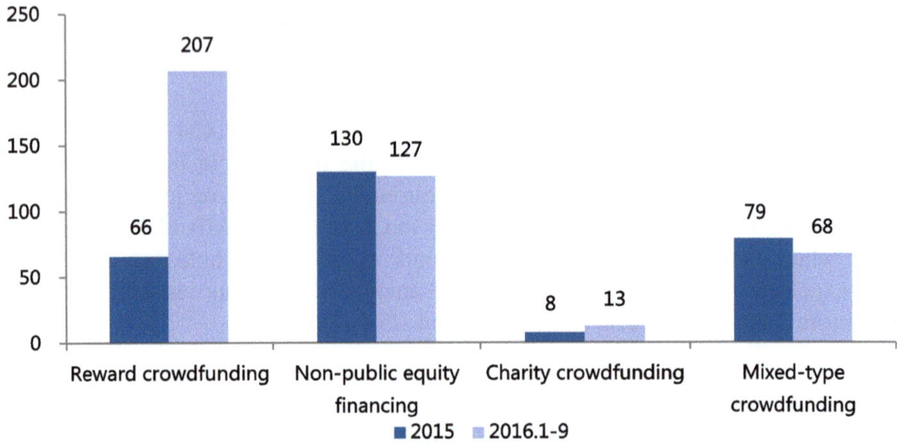

Fig. 2.4 Comparison of different types of crowdfunding platforms in China. *Data Source* www.yingcanzixun.com

2.2.2 *The Successful Crowdfunding Projects*

From January 2016 to September 2016, the crowdfunding industry in China successfully completed 53,600 projects in total, increased by 136.68% compared with the number in the whole year of 2015. Among them, 39,908 are reward crowdfunding projects, 9911 are charity crowdfunding projects, and both of them increased compared with 2015. Meanwhile, 3732 non-public equity financing projects are successfully completed, and the number is basically equal to that of projects successfully completed in 2015 (Fig. 2.5).

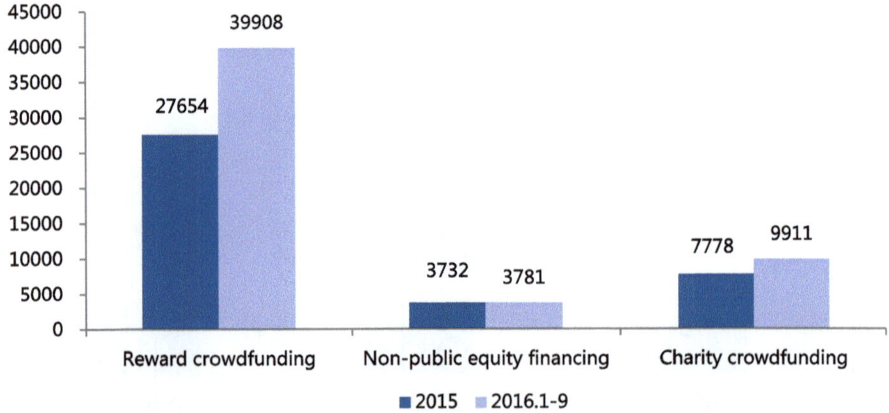

Fig. 2.5 Comparison of various types of successful crowdfunding projects in China. *Data Source* www.yingcanzixun.com

2.2.3 *The Amount of Funds Raised*

From January 2016 to September 2016, the crowdfunding industry in China successfully raised RMB 11.801 billion. Among that, the amount of reward crowdfunding accounts for more than 50%, up to RMB 6.803 billion, which well exceeds the amount of funds successfully raised via reward crowdfunding in the whole year of 2015; the amount of equity crowdfunding reached RMB 4.677 billion, which was about 90.12% of that in 2015; and the amount of charity crowdfunding was less than that of 2015, with RMB 321 million (Fig. 2.6).

2.2.4 *The Number of Crowdfunding Investors*

From January 2016 to September 2016, the number of investors of crowdfunding industry in China reached 85.6048 million, exceeding the number of investors at the end of year 2015. Among them, the number of investors in reward crowdfunding showed fastest growth, reached 42.2123 million; the number of investors in charity crowdfunding in the first nine months of 2016 exceeded that of 2015, even though the amount of funds raised by charity crowdfunding only accounted for 50.87% of that of 2015; as the equity crowdfunding has a higher threshold and stricter policy constraint, only 9800 investors participated during this period of time, which was less than 50% of that of 2015 (Fig. 2.7).

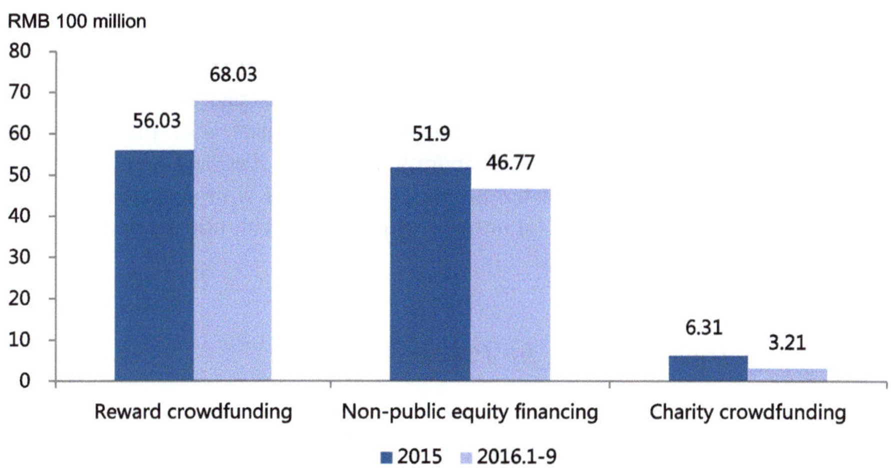

Fig. 2.6 Comparison in amount of funds successfully raised by various types of crowdfunding in China. *Data Source* www.yingcanzixun.com

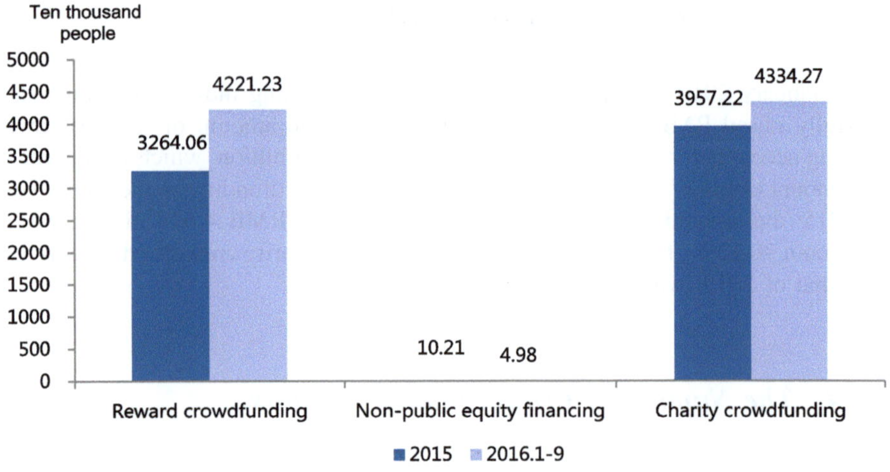

Fig. 2.7 Comparison in number of crowdfunding investors in China. *Data Source* www.yingcanzixun.com

2.3 The Statistics of Regional Development

2.3.1 The Number of Platforms by Provinces

By the end of September 2016, the crowdfunding platforms in China were distributed in 28 provinces/cities, most of which are the economically developed coastal areas. As the earliest development area of crowdfunding, Beijing and Guangdong had obvious "concentration effect", with the largest number of platforms with normal operations in China. According to a quarterly statistics of Yingcanzixun.com, a primary internet finance portal in China, Guangdong ranks the top with 92 platforms; followed by Beijing with 88 platforms; Shandong ranks the third and Shanghai the fourth, with 57 platforms and 49 platforms, respectively; Zhejiang ranks the fifth with 28 platforms; and Jiangsu ranks the sixth with 23 platforms. Guangdong, Beijing, Shandong, Shanghai, Zhejiang and Jiangsu are the top six in China in terms of the number of platforms with normal operations, accounting for 81.20% of the total number of platforms with normal operations all over the country (Fig. 2.8).

2.3.2 Fundraising Scale by Provinces

From January 2016 to September 2016, Beijing, Guangdong and Zhejiang ranked the top three for the amount of funds raised by crowdfunding platforms in China, with funds raised up to RMB 3.772 billion, RMB 2.537 billion and RMB 2.049 billion, respectively. Among them, the amount of funds raised by Guangdong

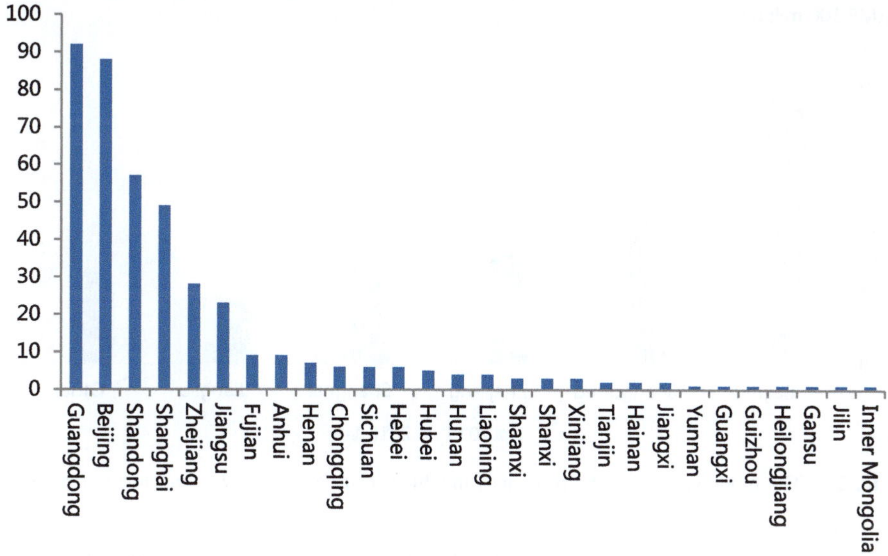

Fig. 2.8 The number of platforms by provinces in China. *Data Source* www.yingcanzixun.com

and Zhejiang exceeded that of 2015. Shanghai ranked the fourth, with the funds raised up to RMB 1.108 billion; and Jiangsu ranked the fifth, with funds raised up to RMB 947 million. The sum of the amount of funds raised by the 5 provinces and cities above accounted for 88.24% of total amount of funds raised by the entire country. These five provinces and cities are the most economically developed areas in China with much stronger investment consciousness and policy support from local governments. As a result, the scale of the crowdfunding in China is expected to be still largely determined by these provinces and cities in a short and medium term. Meanwhile, the other 23 provinces and cities with crowdfunding platforms only raised RMB 1.388 billion in the same period of time with significant regional differences (Fig. 2.9).

2.4 Some Analysis of the Primary Business of Crowdfunding Platforms

2.4.1 The Distribution of Primary Business of Platforms

The primary business of China's crowdfunding platforms can be divided into two categories: one is the comprehensive platform involving multiple industries or fields such as high tech, agricultural products, and film and television, and the examples include JD Crowdfunding and Taobao Crowdfunding. Another one is the more concentrated, professional, and vertical crowdfunding platform, which focuses on sub-industries or fields, such as arts, specific agricultural products, entertainment,

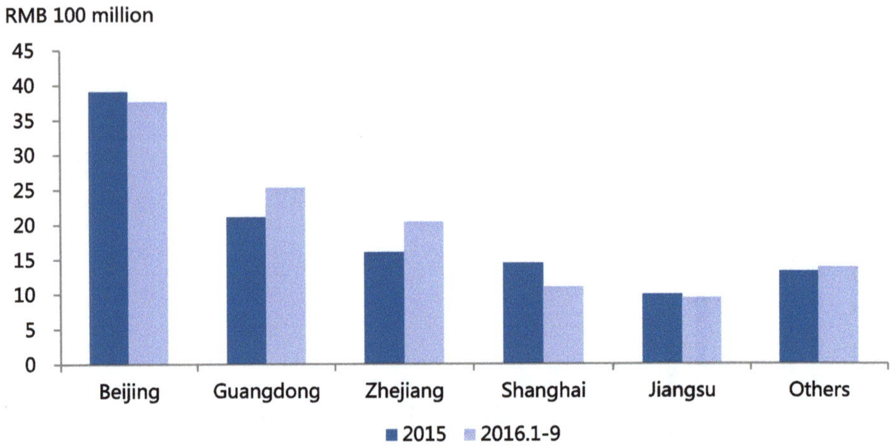

Fig. 2.9 The fundraising scale by provinces in China. *Data Source* www.yingcanzixun.com

automobiles, and real estate. In particular, the platforms focusing on automobile crowdfunding mushroomed in 2016.

According to a quarterly statistics of Yingcanzixun.com, by the end of September 2016, among the 415 crowdfunding platforms with normal operation in China, 241 comprehensive type of platforms ranked the top, accounting for 58.07% of the total platforms, followed by 82 platforms focusing on automobile crowd-funding, accounting for 19.76; 25 platforms focusing on film and television crowdfunding ranked the third, accounting for 6.02%; and 21 platforms focusing on physical store crowdfunding, with a percentage close to the film and television focused platforms; the charity crowdfunding platforms ranked the fifth with 12 platforms, accounting for 3.13% of the total number of platforms; and the real estate focused crowdfunding platforms ranked the sixth with 12 ones; however, due to some policy related reasons, some of these platforms temporarily stopped updating their information. In addition, there were also 10 agricultural focused crowdfunding platforms, and 1–2 other vertical crowdfunding platforms in some subdivided fields (Fig. 2.10).

2.4.2 Some Analysis of Projects of Comprehensive Platforms

According to a quarterly statistics of Yingcanzixun.com, by the end of September 2016, the crowdfunding platforms, as indicated earlier, are more inclined to involve in multiple business fields simultaneously. Among the 241 comprehensive plat-forms, 53 platforms involved in agriculture, primarily agricultural products; 40 platforms conducted physical store projects; 36 platforms participated in charity crowdfunding; 27 platforms dabbed in film and television projects; and only 5

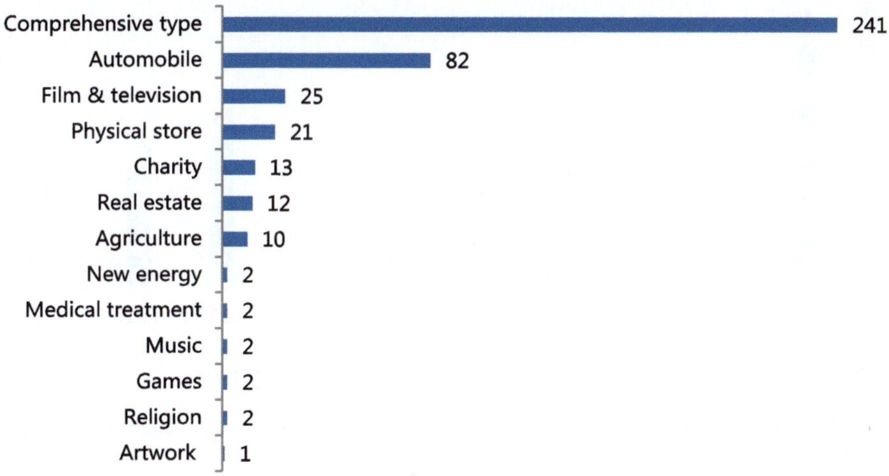

Fig. 2.10 Distribution of concentrations of the platforms. *Data Source* www.yingcanzixun.com

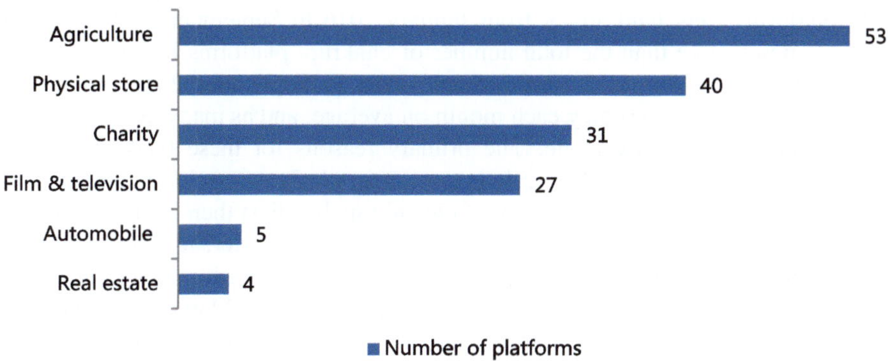

Fig. 2.11 Analysis of projects of comprehensive platforms. *Data Source* www.yingcanzixun.com

comprehensive platforms listed automobile projects, and 4 platforms posted real estate projects. It can be seen that the automobile and real estate projects are more likely financed through these more specialized vertical platforms. In contrast, agricultural products crowdfunding are generally conducted through comprehensive platforms, instead of vertical platforms (Fig. 2.11).

2.5 The Analysis of Bankrupt and Transformed Platforms

According to a quarterly statistics of Yingcanzixun, from 2015 to the end of September 2016, 174 crowdfunding platforms went bankruptcy (i.e. the platform's website cannot be opened for more than 30 days or crowdfunding module no longer

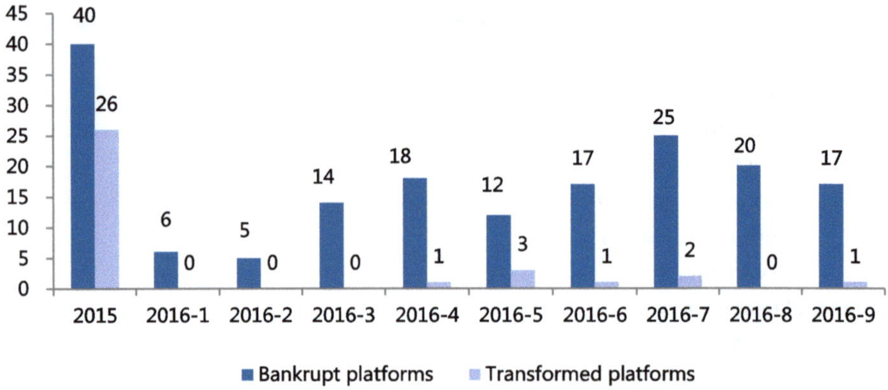

Fig. 2.12 Number of bankrupt and transformed platforms: 2015–January 2016. *Data Source* www.yingcanzixun.com

exists), and 34 crowdfunding platforms are transformed to non-crowdfunding platforms. For these bankrupt platforms, 40 platforms went bankrupt in 2015, and 134 platforms went bankruptcy from January 2016 to September 2016, which is about 3 times more than the total number of bankrupt platforms in 2015.

As showed in Fig. 2.12, from March 2016 to September 2016, more than 10 platforms went bankruptcy each month on average, and as many as 25 platforms went bankruptcy in July alone. The primary reasons for these bankruptcies are found to be that, with a smaller scale in size, these platforms couldn't compete with these giant platforms in resources, but failed to timely adjust their business focuses. When the policies towards the crowdfunding became stricter, it was difficult for these platforms to continue their operations. It would be worth mentioning that an important contributing factor for more bankruptcy between March and September in 2016 is the policy change during that period of time. As mentioned in earlier sections, policies issued then prohibited real estate crowdfunding, and P2P online lending platforms were not allowed to be engaged in equity crowdfunding, either. As a result, many P2P online lending platforms took out their crowdfunding modules, and crowdfunding platforms removed their real estate modules. In addition, the bankruptcy of these platforms is also related to the special rectification and investigation of internet finance industry taken by regulators. For these transformed crowdfunding platforms, the post-transformed businesses primarily include: P2P online lending, peripheral services of crowdfunding, entrepreneurial trainings, social networks, group purchases, e-trading, lottery, product supplier, and advisory service for wealth management products.

Chapter 3
The Basic Model Analysis of Crowdfunding in China

Zhi Chen and Haimei Wang

3.1 The Reward Crowdfunding

As defined earlier, reward crowdfunding is a type of fundraising using physical products, services, and rights and benefits as a return to investors, and is also the most popular type of crowdfunding in China at present. There are 207 reward crowdfunding platforms so far in China, which involve in the industries of smart hardware, agriculture, used cars, and film and television, with various forms of return to investors.

3.1.1 The Procedures of Reward Crowdfunding

For most platforms, such as JD Crowdfunding and Taobao Crowdfunding, the procedures of reward crowdfunding can be described as follows, and summarized in Fig. 3.1.

1. Crowdfunding platform will review the submitted products or projects from the product or project initiators. If approved, the platform will post it online; if not, the platform will cancel the project.
2. For the approved projects, the platform will communicate with the product or project initiators for documentation and design. After it settled, the project will go online, and the crowdfunding towards potential investors will start.
3. Within the pre-specified period of time, if crowdfunding is successful, the platform will transfer the initial funds to the project initiators; if failed, the platforms will return the collected funds to the investors.

Z. Chen (✉) · H. Wang
Shanghai Wenxi Investment Consulting Co., Shanghai, China
e-mail: chenzhi@wdzj.com

J.G. Wang et al. (eds.), *Financing from Masses*,
https://doi.org/10.1007/978-981-10-5843-1_3

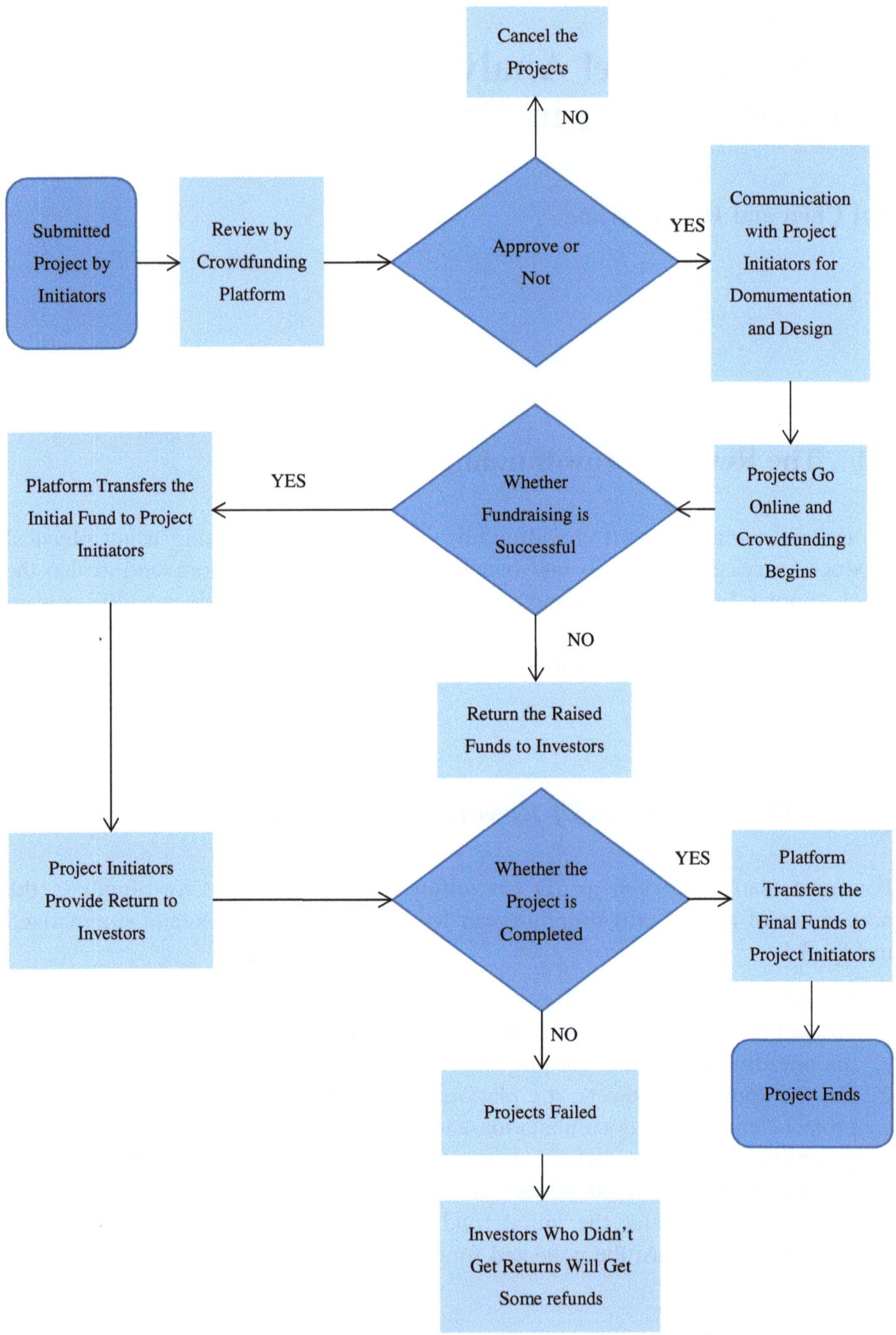

Fig. 3.1 Procedures of reward crowdfunding. *Data Source* www.yingcanzixun.com

4. The project initiators who successfully obtained funds shall pay the promised returns to investors within the pre-specified period of time. If investors received the returns as promised, then the platform will transfer the remaining or final funds to the project initiators, and the project successfully ends; if the project initiators fail to provide the investors with the returns as promised, then the project failed, and the investors who didn't receive the promised returns will get some refunds.

Compared with the procedure above, there is an additional follow-up procedure for Suning Crowdfunding after the normal procedure of reward crowdfunding is completed. Relying on its many widely spread physical stores, Suning also facilitates resales for the products with successful crowdfunding. The procedure with resale process can be described as follows, and shown in Fig. 3.2.

1. For the products with successful crowdfunding, the platform will conduct resale assessment. The resale schedule will be determined if the product passed the assessment, and the resale will start; otherwise, the resale will be canceled.
2. Product provider will submit the application to Suning stores for product display. If approved, Suning will select stores for display and resale with a period of 3–6 months; otherwise, the application will be denied, and the display will not occur.
3. The return can be obtained for the investors within the resale period. Product provider will make a settlement every 1–2 weeks within the resale period. If the return is not paid as promised, the resale failed, and the investors can receive a refund with additional 5% compensation.
4. After the resale ends, the product provider can apply for getting their resale product to be sold offline in Suning stores. If the application succeeds, the product will be sold in Suning stores; otherwise, product provider ends the project.

3.1.2 *The Profit Model of Reward Crowdfunding Platforms*

From a global perspective, almost all the mainstream crowdfunding platforms take a proportion of the total amount of raised funds for successful projects as the commission to the platforms, under the name of crowdfunding service fee, which is the main source of platform's cash inflow so far. For example, JD Crowdfunding and Suning Crowdfunding charge 3% of total amount of raised funds as the service fee, and Zhongchou charges 1.5% of total amount raised as the service fee, while Taobao Crowdfunding is considered an exception for providing crowdfunding service free. Crowdfunding platforms, investors, and the project initiators basically reach a consensus: service fee is collected only for the successfully funded projects. Otherwise, the crowdfunding platforms will return the raised funds to the investors without any charges.

After crowdfunding succeeds, different platforms will transfer different amount of initial funds to the project initiators. JD Crowdfunding and Zhongchou pay the

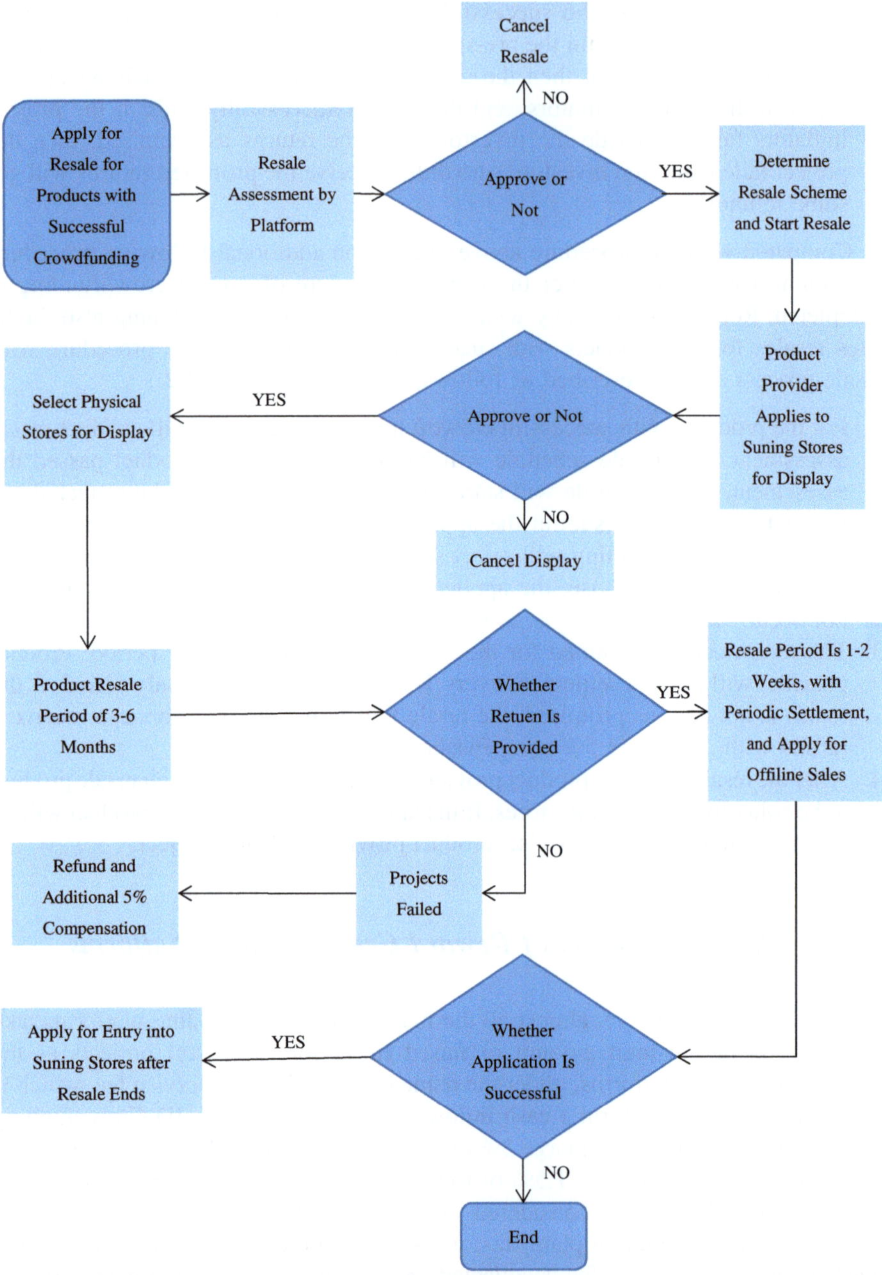

Fig. 3.2 Resale procedures of suning crowdfunding projects after crowdfunding ends. *Data Source* www.yingcanzixun.com

Table 3.1 Charges and initial payments for reward crowdfunding platforms

Platform	Service fee	Proportion of initial payment
Taobao crowdfunding	Free	50% of total raised funds
JD crowdfunding	3% of total raised funds	70% of total raised funds after deduction of service fee
Suning crowdfunding	3% of total raised funds	60% of total raised funds after deduction of service fee
Zhongchou	1.5% of total raised funds	70% of total raised funds after deduction of service fee

Data Source www.yingcanzixun.com

highest proportion of the total funds needed, up to 70%, as the initial payment, while Suning Crowdfunding pays 60%, and Taobao Crowdfunding pays 50%, respectively. Only after the investors confirm the receipt of the promised products, the platforms will transfer the remaining balance to the project initiators.

The less the service fee, the lower the financial pressure undertaken by the project initiator; the lower the proportion of the initial payments, the safer for the investors to be protected, because that, if the crowdfunding succeeds but financed projects fails, the investors can request for refund of all remaining funds that are unpaid to the project initiators yet. The portion of the payback of the initial payment needs to be negotiated by related parties (Table 3.1).

In addition to commissions or service fees, the reward crowdfunding platforms also take their platforms' advantages and offline resources to provide professional consulting services or incubating services, and charge some related service fees. Some crowdfunding platforms also attempt to get more internet flow or "traffic" using their platforms' influence to generate some joint marketing and advertisement revenues.

3.1.3 The Risks of Reward Crowdfunding

Several types of risks related with the reward crowdfunding have been identified as follows:

(1) Moral Risk

As most crowdfunding products are new products, which may naturally have many flaws. Project initiators may actually use investors' funding to run a new product test.

(2) Capital Risk

If crowdfunding funds have been invested into the production of the proposed products, but production of product fails, the investors may not be able to get their full amount of invested fund back.

(3) Lack of Post-Sales Services

Most project initiating firms that launched crowdfunding are not mature or experienced enterprises. The post-sales services may not be in place if any quality or software issues incurred.

(4) Sales Risk

If the crowdfunding is only used as an alternative way of sales by the producer, so investors may not actually receive any real "investment returns" as they may expect.

(5) Legal Risk

All crowdfunding products may involve in legal issues such as infringement, plagiarism and violation of regulations, so the investors may be negatively impacted when it occurred.

3.1.4 Some Case Analysis of Reward Crowdfunding Projects

The success of crowdfunding projects depend highly upon the innovation, brand development and promotion, and use of social media software. The most critical factor for the success of a reward crowdfunding is the creativity, intelligence and characteristics of the projects. It is almost impossible for a project without its uniqueness and creativities to obtain the favor of the investors.

In addition, the success of crowdfunding of a project does not imply the success of the funded project. For the reward crowdfunding, after the funds are successfully raised, the projects may still encounter many issues, such as delayed product release, large discrepancy between the actual product quality/features and the previous descriptions, and failure of the project. As a result, the investors may not be able to receive the expected returns. For example, in the event of bankruptcy of Dakele Mobile Phone,[1] the crowdfunding succeeded but the project failed, and the investors ended up with nothing. What's even more are there no regulations on reward crowdfunding in China now. As a result, the potential investors may need to fully understand that the reward crowdfunding is truly a type of "investment", which inherited the risk that any investment may bear, and it is not a form of "group purchase + pre-sale", as may be misunderstood by many participants.

[1]http://it.sohu.com/20160310/n439955530.shtml.

(1) Some Successful Cases

Monkey King: Hero is Back

The most popular animated film in China in 2015 should be nothing but Monkey King: Hero is Back.[2] This film recorded box revenue RMB 925 million within 62 days since it was released. The names of 109 investors that appeared at the end of the film makes the business model behind the film received excessive attentions from the general public. As reported, Lu Wei, the producer of the movie started crowdfunding by sending out a message of fundraising via his WeChat. Eventually, 89 investors participated, and the 109 names that appeared at the end of the film are just the names of the children of these 89 investors. Totally, RMB 7.89 million funds were raised, and RMB 30 million of principal and interest were finally paid back to the investors, with nearly RMB 250,000 gain for each investor on average.

The success of the movie is not an accident. It took eight years to complete the production of the film, with various promotion activities such as endorsement of entertainment stars, WeChat circulations, and Weibo discussions. With these joint efforts, the movie became known to general public and eventually received support from audiences. Its success is not only a milestone for China's domestic animation film, but also a bench mark for film and television crowdfunding. It demonstrates how a concrete crowdfunding project can be successfully worked out. Monkey King: Hero is Back is not the first experiment of film and television crowdfunding in China, but it truly educated the general public for this innovative way of financing and investment, and enabled the potential investors to participate in the this new path of investment with internet + project + crowdfunding.

Galaxy S6 Edge

On June 12, 2015, Galaxy S6 Edge Phones started fundraising online on crowdfunding platforms.[3] As only 1600 Galaxy S6 Edge phones will be sold through JD Crowdfunding, therefore, not all the investors who participated in crowdfunding are guaranteed to get a phone. JD Crowdfunding provides four buying options for investors/buyers, including "RMB 1 Rush Purchase", "Original Cost within 1 s", "Auction within Limited Time", and "Open Competitive Purchase". As reported, within 1 s after the phones came online, 23 investors participated in rush purchase simultaneously. By the end of the fundraising period, 359,592 investors participated in crowdfunding, and RMB 9.811 million was raised, which is 3270% of the original target.

The reason for the popularity of Galaxy S6 Edge phones could be attributed to its well-designed appearance, the words "Iron Man", and the limited edition, all of which attracted the fans of Samsung and Marvel. In addition, each mobile phone will have its exclusive code, which pertains collection value for the digital code

[2]Online Lending House: Annual selection: The most creative and popular projects of crowdfunding industry of China. January 12, 2016, http://www.wdzj.com/news/zhongchou/25766.html.

[3]JD Finance: Galaxy S6 Edge, http://z.jd.com/project/details/14151.html.

freaks and fans of Marvel. Meanwhile, Samsung launched H5 interactive games online, which allowed the interaction with consumers and further expanded the promotion. With the joint effort of the brand effect of Samsung, the "fans effect" of Marvel, and the "word of mouth" promotion among consumers via social media networks, Galaxy S6 Edge became the crowdfunding project with the highest investor participation in crowdfunding history in China.

(2) A Failed Case

Pepsi Mobile Phone
On November 18, 2015, Pepsi Mobile Phone launched its crowdfunding,[4] and planned to raise RMB 3 million between November 18 and December 3. Even though the amount of raised funds reached RMB 600,000 up to the second day of crowdfunding, by the end of the pre-specified fundraising period, Pepsi Mobile Phone only raised RMB 1.3 million in total, about 43% of the target. As a result, the failure of crowdfunding was announced.

The failure of Pepsi Mobile Phone may not be caused by lack of attention from general public. As a well-known brand, it is an eye-catching news itself that Pepsi will make mobile phones, and it did obtain support of 12,152 investors with funding of RMB 1.3 million. However, its failure may come from its over-excess valuation and high fundraising target. In particular, Pepsi didn't participate in the design, production, and crowdfunding of the mobile phones, except for providing a brand, and there is no special and innovative features of the proposed mobile phones. So it appears that the "netizens" won't purchase anything if the products don't possess any innovative features with values, even though it is under a well-known brand name.

3.2 Equity Crowdfunding or Non-public Equity Financing

Equity crowdfunding or non-public equity financing, as discussed earlier, is the exchange of shares of a private company for capital from investors. Investors who participate in the crowdfunding typically take the format of "leading + following investment". Under this model, investors will join the project initiators, who are generally the start-up entrepreneurs, to undertake risks and share benefits together. Currently, there are 127 equity crowdfunding platforms in China.

[4]Online Lending House: 2015 Top 10 events of crowdfunding industry of China, February 12, 2016, http://www.wdzj.com/news/zhongchou/25768.html.

3.2.1 *The Procedures of Equity Crowdfunding*

(1) The Procedure of "Leading + Following Investment"

The "leading + following investment" is the mainstream model of equity crowdfunding platforms at present that are adopted by many major equity crowdfunding platforms such Zhongtou8. The regular procedure of this business model is as follows:

1. A Project initiator submits the project application online;
2. Platform staffs review the projects, and post the projects online after the submitted projects passed the review;
3. Projects, then, enter into the stage of subscription for investors. Potential investors will view the projects, and interview the project initiators offline, if they are interested in the projects. Finally, they will determine the leading investors, introduce following investors, and settle for the investment intention and amount of funds that need to be raised;
4. Within the pre-specified period of time, if the fund raised reaches or exceeds the expected financing target, then online funding procedure ends. Project initiators will select the final investors among the ones who expressed investment intention. If the fundraising fails, all contributed funds and management fees paid by investors will be returned back to the investors in full amount; or, if the amount of raised funds reaches a certain ratio of the original target, investors may negotiate with the project initiators on whether they can revise the initial fundraising plan for the target number, and re-sign an investment agreement according to the actually raised funds and the corresponding equity shares;
5. After the crowdfunding succeeds, investors will transfer funds into the designated account of the project initiators;
6. When the funds transferred, the related parties will begin to process some documentation and registration issues, such as setting up limited partnerships, and changing the titles of industrial and commercial registrations;
7. Post-investment service will be provided by the platforms to allow investors to interact with the project initiators directly, and monitor the operations of the funded firms in real time;
8. Exit from the investment (Fig. 3.3).

(2) Procedures of "Speed Dating" Crowdfunding

"Speed Dating" is an innovative way of crowdfunding for some equity crowdfunding platforms, such as AngelCrunch,[5] with large scale and many projects online. It provides the project initiators with a much more efficient way to obtain investment through offline roadshow to potential investors. Its specific procedure is as follows.

[5]http://angelcrunch.com/.

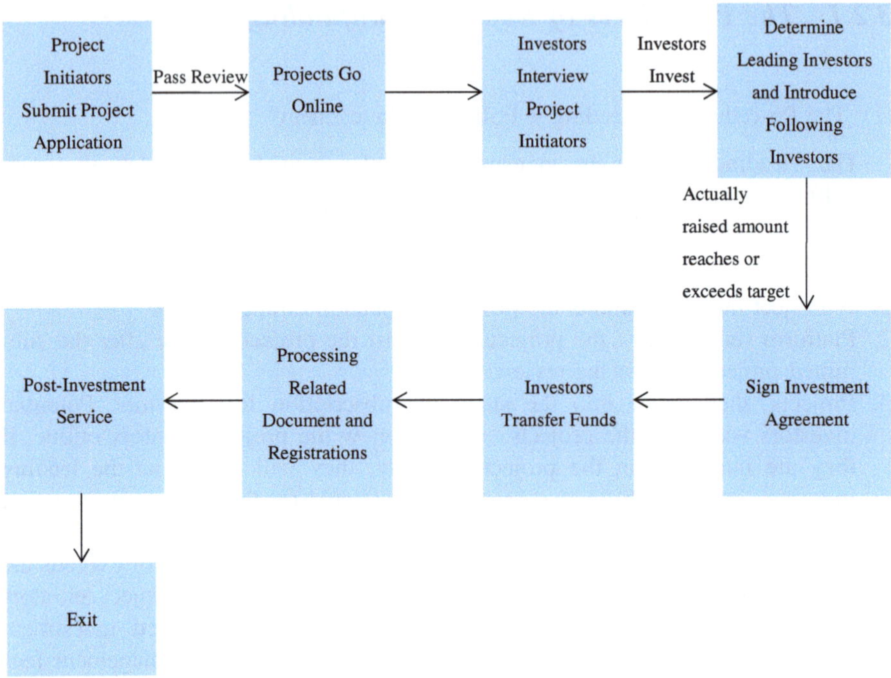

Fig. 3.3 The procedures of non-public equity crowdfunding. *Data Source* www.yingcanzixun.com

1. The project initiators register online to participate in "speed dating";
2. The platforms screen projects for the preliminary selection of the projects;
3. The platforms further review the projects that passed the preliminary selection, and finalize the projects to be posted online;
4. The platforms will help project initiators prepare the roadshow, including the roadshow agenda, organization of the presentation materials, training on presentation skills, and a rehearsal one or two days before the formal roadshow;
5. "Speed Dating": The selected projects will be presented intensively within a half day or so with a Q&A session. The interested investors will meet with the project initiators, typically, in the afternoon of the day. If it works out, the both parties will sign the investment agreement right away. The whole process can generally be completed within one day.
6. Financing is completed.

The above process can be visualized through the chart below:

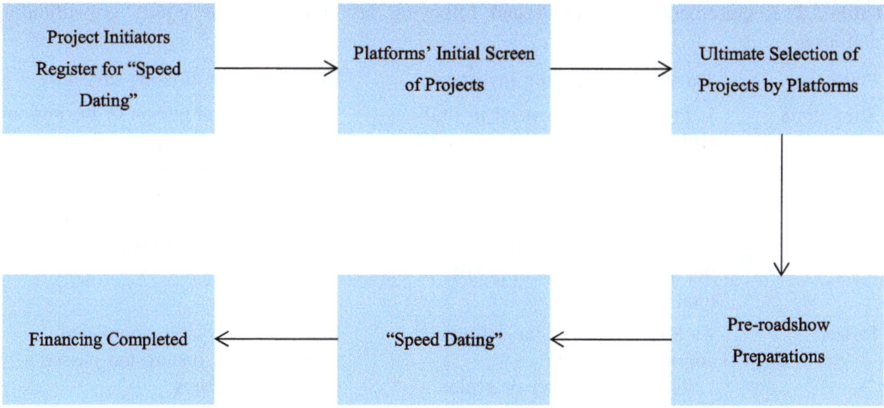

The procedure of "speed dating". *Data Source* www.yingcanzixun.com

3.2.2 *The Investor Threshold of Equity Crowdfunding*

The thresholds for investors and investment amount in the equity crowdfunding, due to its special nature, are quite different from that of the reward crowdfunding or the charity crowdfunding, which, basically, have no threshold at all.

Under the "leading + following investment" model of the equity crowdfunding, there are some strict requirements set up by almost all the platforms for leading investors, such as some rigid requirements on net assets, or financial assets, or investor's annual income, whether the investors are professional investors or professional financial institutions, whether the investors have the investment skills and post-investment management ability, whether the investors have the experience of successful exit, and whether they have adequate experiences in certain industries or fields. However, the requirements for "following investors" vary by platforms. Some platforms only require the following investors to register with his/her real name and passes the basic evaluations. But some platforms may require some thresholds that are similar to that of the "leading" investors, such as annual income, financial assets, or net assets, and the qualifications of professional financial institutions or professional investors (Table 3.2).

3.2.3 *The Business Model of Equity Crowdfunding*

Equity crowdfunding or non-public equity financing developed rapidly in recent years in China, and attracted attentions of both investors and project initiators. Due to the higher risk and higher threshold of equity investment, however, the success rate of equity crowdfunding is generally low, and the equity crowdfunding

Table 3.2 Requirements on leading and following investors of some equity crowdfunding platforms

Platform	Threshold of leading investors	Threshold of following investors
Zhongtou8	1. Professional financial institutions ranked top 200 by Zero2IPO VC Firms 2. For each project, the minimum amount of leading investment is 20% of the total funds raised, and the maximum amount is 50% of the total funds raised	1. Valid natural person or institution in China, with adequate adopting capability to possible existing risks 2. The minimum amount of following investment for each project is RMB 100,000
Ibstart	As long as any of the following conditions is met: 1. The actual owner or senior executive of listed companies, the private equity funds registered in the securities association and the actual owner or senior executives of these institutions, as well as the investors who held a position as the manager of Angel Fund, VC and PE Fund and above, and have deep understanding and judgment ability for relevant industries 2. Well-known enterprise founders 3. Well-known investors 4. The paid-in capital of institutional investors shall not be less than RMB 30 million	Investors who have completed registration in Ibstart and passed background check
36 Kr	1. Angel investors or professional leading investment institutions with the experience of successful exit 2. Fully agree to the development principle and direction of the platform 3. Have rich experience in a certain industry or field, independent judgment ability, abundant industry resources and influence, as well as strong risk-identifying ability 4. Have investment management ability and post-investment management ability	Pass the real name authentication of the platform and meet any of the following conditions: 1. Personal financial assets exceed RMB 1 million 2. Annual income exceed RMB 300,000 3. Professional venture capital personnel working in investment institutions
Dajiatou	As long as any of the following conditions is met 1. Have at least two years of work experience at the post of the manager of Angel Fund, primary VC Fund and posts above 2. Have at least two years of entrepreneurial experience (only	Register for angle investor to obtain the qualification for following investment of projects

(continued)

Table 3.2 (continued)

Platform	Threshold of leading investors	Threshold of following investors
	limited to experience of the first founder) 3. Have at least three years of work experience at the post of corporate director and posts above 4. Have at least five years of work experience at the post of corporate manager 5. Have at least two cases of angle investment	
Touhu	1. Leading investors shall have invested at least three projects, and shall have successful investment cases. The standards for those who have successful investment cases can be looser 2. Leading investors shall have certain influence in project-related fields and shall have rich industry experience and industry resources 3. Leading investors shall have stronger independent judgment capability and risk-resisting capability, and shall have strong spirit of sharing 4. Leading investors shall be the active investors in Touhu (who have invested projects in recent six months and negotiated on projects in the latest month) 5. Leading investors shall have enough time to help projects develop, can professionally assist entrepreneurs to carry out follow-up work, such as improving business planning, determining valuation, investment clauses and financing amount, assist in project roadshow and bring industry resources and experience for projects, and fully promote following investment and financing of this round	Any of the following conditions shall be met 1. Professional investment institutions or professional investors 2. Personal average annual income of the recent three years shall not be less than RMB 500,000 3. Financial assets shall not be less than RMB 3 million
Yunchou	1. Have financial assets more than RMB 1 million, or net assets more than RMB 3 million, or annual income more than RMB 500,000 2. The profession is professional investor, or investment posts of	1. Investors shall reach 18 years old 2. Have personal assets 3. Have the consciousness of investment risk

(continued)

Table 3.2 (continued)

Platform	Threshold of leading investors	Threshold of following investors
	investment institutions, or enterprise director 3. There is at least one project completing investment settlement 4. The amount of leading investment of leading investors needs to reach a certain proportion (at least 30%), and leading investors need to conduct due diligence to project party Investment institutions shall meet the following conditions for applying for leading investors: 1. Have professional knowledge of equity investment and corresponding ability, as well as independent risk-identifying capability 2. Units with net assets no less than RMB 10 million 3. Have at least two equity investment cases with the investment amount for each project exceeding RMB 1 million 4. Have the exit experience of more than one project, and the investment return shall not be less than 150%	
JD Dongjia	1. Fully agree to the development principle and direction of Dongjia 2. Have rich experience in a certain industry or field, independent judgment ability, abundant industry resources and influence, as well as strong risk-bearing ability 3. Have investment management ability and post-investment management ability 4. Leading investors have at least one projects non-listed equity investment projects which have exited, or leading investors have the experience of independent successful venture pioneering 5. Be diligent and duteous and willing to share	1. Individual qualified investors shall meet any of the following conditions: (1) The average annual income of the recent three years shall not be less than RMB 300,000 (2) Have financial assets no less than RMB 1 million. Financial assets include bank deposit, stock, securities, fund share, asset management plan, bank financial product, trust plan, insurance products and futures interest 2. Qualified unit investors shall meet the following conditions: (1) The minimum amount invested for a single financing project shall not be less than RMB 100,000 (2) For pension fund such as social security fund and enterprise annuity, social non-profit fund like charitable fund, as well as investment plan set or recorded according to the

(continued)

Table 3.2 (continued)

Platform	Threshold of leading investors	Threshold of following investors
		requirements of financial regulation department, the investors foregoing are exempted from penetrating check and the number of investors is aggregated
AngelCrunch	1. Leading investors shall meet the requirements for qualified investors of AngleCrunch 2. Leading investors shall be the active investors of AngleCrunch (who have invested projects in recent six months and negotiated on projects in the latest month) 3. Have rich experience in a certain field, independent judgment ability, abundant industry resources and influence, as well as strong risk-bearing ability 4. Lead to invest in no more than 5 projects in one year, have sufficient time to help projects develop 5. There is at least one project exiting 6. Be able to professionally assist projects to improve BP, determine valuation, investment clauses and financing amount, assist in project roadshow and complete following investment and financing of this round 7. Have strong spirit of sharing, and be willing to share the leaded projects to other investors	1. Natural person investors shall meet any of the following conditions (1) The investors' average annual income of the recent three years shall exceed RMB 300,000, or the couple's average annual income of the recent three years shall exceed RMB 600,000, and relevant income certificate can be provided (2) The market value of the financial assets under the name of investors shall be more than RMB 1 million. Financial assets include bank deposit, stock, securities, fund share, asset management plan, bank financial product, trust plan, insurance products and futures interest. And relevant asset certificate can be provided (3) The financial value of the fixed assets under the name of investors shall be more than RMB 5 million, excluding the primary residence. And relevant property certificate can be provided (4) Investors shall have the investment cases with angle investment more than RMB 100,000 in TMT field, and can provide relevant investment case certificate 2. Institutions shall meet any of the following conditions (1) The paid-in registered capital of companies and enterprises shall exceed RMB 10 million (2) The total assets/management assets of companies and enterprises shall exceed RMB 30 million, and relevant property certificate can be provided (3) The net profit of companies and enterprises of the recent three years shall not be less than RMB 5

(continued)

Table 3.2 (continued)

Platform	Threshold of leading investors	Threshold of following investors
		million, and relevant property certificate can be provided (4) Companies and enterprises shall have the investment cases with angle investment more than RMB 300,000 in TMT field, and can provide relevant investment case certificate
Choudao Equity	1. Fully agree to the development principle and direction of the platform 2. Have rich experience in a certain industry or field, independent judgment ability, abundant industry resources and influence, as well as strong risk-bearing ability 3. Have investment management ability and post-investment management ability 4. Be diligent and duteous	1. Units with net assets not less than RMB 5 million 2. Individuals with financial assets no less than RMB 500,000 or the personal average annual income of the recent years no less than RMB 200,000

Data Source www.yingcanzixun.com

platforms face the challenges of making profit. At present, equity crowdfunding platforms primarily adopt three types of business models:

(1) The Commission-Based Model

The commission-based model is the most commonly used model in the industry at the current stage. Under this model, the platforms will charge a commission as a certain percentage of the total funds raised, if the crowdfunding succeeds. There is no fixed ratio, and the percentage charged varies among the platforms, which is usually 3–5% of the total funds raised.

(2) The Equity Shares Model

Under equity shares model, the platforms do not charge commission from the project initiators directly, instead, they require certain shares of the funded firm as a return. This model is typically used in financing start-ups at the "seed" or "angle" investment stage. The common practice of most platforms at the current stage is to combine commission model and equity shares model. The platforms still take the commission, but will invest part or all of the commission in the funded firms to become the shareholder of the firm.

(3) The Value-Added Service Fee Model

Under this model, equity crowdfunding platforms will provide various value-added services for the project initiators, and charge fees for these value-added services, such as incubator service, financial advisory service, and legal service.

3.2.4 The Risks of Equity Crowdfunding

There are several risks that were identified for the equity crowdfunding as follows:

(1) Legitimacy of Equity Crowdfunding

As an activity to collect money from general public, under the current security laws and regulations in China, there is a possibility for some crowdfunding activities to be considered illegal, if they are classified by regulators as illegally collecting public funds and illegally issuing financial securities.

(2) Non-standardized Review Mechanism for the Projects to be Funded

The projects submitted by project initiators will be reviewed by the platforms before their posting online for the investors. The platforms play a role of "filter" to pre-qualify the projects that required funding from investors. However, as the newly developed industry, the criterion used by various platforms may vary, and these criterion are not standardized and less transparent with adequate monitoring.

(3) Investors Lack Professional Investment Ability

While crowdfunding relatively lowers down the entry barrier for equity investment by allowing smaller investors to join the game, it also brings much more less-prepared, non-professional investors into the door. Those non-professional investors, typically, lack the needed knowledge for equity investment, and, less likely, they can properly identify the right projects to invest, which will undoubtedly lead to the higher probability of loss of their investment.

(4) Risk of Entrusting-Shareholding

For the financing through equity crowdfunding, most demanding project initiating firms are limited partnerships. According to the provision of Article 24 of China's Company Law, "A limited liability company shall be invested in and established by no more than 50 shareholders."[6] Therefore, the crowdfunding projects cannot have more than 50 shareholders in the registration if taking limited partnership as the business form. However, the funds required by the project initiators may not be adequately provided by only 50 investors, as a result, entrusting-shareholding arrangement may be required for actually involving in more investors, and consequently, the risk associated with the entrusting share-holding, such as no legal status in the registration, misrepresentation by actual owner's representatives, and the law suits or death of the representatives of the actual owners, may occur.

(5) Difficulty in Early Exit

The typical ways of exit from equity crowdfunding are dividend payout, merge and acquisition, and IPO. As the funded firms are, typically, in the early stage of their development, it is, usually, less likely for such firms to be able to declare any

[6]http://www.npc.gov.cn/wxzl/gongbao/2014-03/21/content_1867695.htm.

dividends, and it also may need to take at least 3–5 years for these firms to become a target of merge and acquisition, or to be listed in the equity market. On the other hand, as the smaller investors, the fund providers may not have adequate financial resources to stay in these funded firms for too long. As a result, it would be difficult for the smaller investors to take early exit, and may incur the financial risk for these smaller investors.

3.2.5 Some Case Analysis of Equity Crowdfunding

Equity crowdfunding investors value the most of the prospective market and business model of projects, or simply put, the future profitability and development potentials. Here are some examples of equity crowdfunding.

WiFi Master Key
On May 29, 2015, WiFi Master Key, a company that provides free service for users to identify the free WiFi networks anywhere in nearby local areas, launched a financing plan on equity crowdfunding platforms.[7] The original financing target was to raise RMB 32.5 million with transfer of 0.5% of the firm's shares to investors. However, as the number of subscribers turned out to be significantly exceeding the expected target, the financing plan was changed to raise RMB 65 million with transfer of 1% of the company's shares. The project web page was viewed by more than 100,000 viewers within 1 h after the project went online, and the total amount of subscription intention reached RMB 500 million within 2 h. By the end of the pre-specified fundraising period, the project attracted totally more than 3 million viewers, and 5713 potential investors subscribed totally RMB 7.7142 billion for investment, which was 118 times of the original target, and the project became the one with the highest subscribed funds in China.

As a "sharing-economy" type of company, WiFi Master Key was valuated at USD $1 billion in the previous A-round financing and enjoyed high popularity in the market. So the crowdfunding, as an investment opportunity open to general public, attracted a large number of investors including many loyal users of WiFi Master Key, who love the company, and believe the future of WiFi Master Key. The WiFi Master Key's case showed that the investors prefer the projects that already had obtained external funds earlier with relatively mature business models and higher popularity, and they believe that the probability of successful exit for these projects would be much higher. At the same time, WiFi Master Key's case also demonstrated that there are adequate funds and investors in the equity crowdfunding market, and the scarce resources are the innovative projects with great potentials.

[7]Online Lending House. Annual selection: The most creative and popular project of crowdfunding industry of China. January 12, 2016, http://www.wdzj.com/news/zhongchou/25766.html.

Atzuche

In April 2016, Atzuche, a "sharing-economy" type of car rental company, went online and launched crowdfunding,[8] and the financing target was set up at the range between RMB 25 million and RMB 100 million. It turned out that the amount of funds raised exceeded the lower bound of the targeting range within 3 min after it went online. By the end of the fundraising period, Atzuche successfully raised RMB 95.511 million, near its upper bound of RMB 100 million, which renewed a record of the highest funds raised through crowdfunding in China then.

Similar to WiFi Master Key, Atzuche also received A-round and B-round financing earlier, and many previous investors are large financial institutions such as Matrix Partners China, China Pacific Insurance Company, and CITIC Construction Investment. Apparently, Atchuzu's successful crowdfunding are related, at least partially, to the endorsement of these institutional investors. Of course, the business model of sharing idle cars of Atzuche also attracts wide range of investors. Once again, Atzuche's case showed that the projects with innovative concept and previous funding are the most favorite ones for the investors.

3.2.6 The Entry of Five Internet Giants into Equity Crowdfunding

Equity crowdfunding expands the financing options of the traditional capital market by lowering down the threshold of investment for smaller investors, and providing new fundraising channels for start-ups and small companies with innovative projects. As of the end of September 2016, all the internet giants in China, such as JD, Alibaba, Suning, Baidu and Qihoo 360, had entered into the equity crowdfunding industry by setting up the equity crowdfunding platforms that serve the firms for their needs of fundraising, talent recruiting, and resources collecting, and also help these internet giants themselves select high-quality projects for investment or merger and acquisition.

According to the statistics released by Yingcanzixun, a third party internet finance portal, there were 127 equity crowdfunding platforms under normal operations in China by the end of September 2016, increasing by 6 times compared with 20 platforms in 2014. As predicted by World Bank,[9] by year 2025, the total crowdfunding investment in developing countries around the world will reach USD $96 billion, and China is expected to reach USD $46–$50 billion. Among them, about 70–80% of fund raised will come from equity crowdfunding. At present, sharing economy, entrepreneurship, and innovation represent the most important

[8]Netease News: An App raises RMB 8 million within 3 min through crowdfunding, May 12, 2016, http://news.163.com/16/0512/02/BMR6989500014Q4P.html.

[9]Sun Cheng. Equity crowdfunding has risks, how about purchasing insurance? June 29, 2016, http://www.tmtpost.com/2391491.html.

trends in the market place in China. Equity crowdfunding, as an investment with relatively higher threshold among other crowdfunding forms, the qualified investors are relatively limited, and the development of the equity crowdfunding platforms are relatively healthy without uncontrollable growth, as happened earlier in other internet finance areas such as P2P online lending. As a result, it provides a window opportunity for internet giants, which possess all needed financial and other resources, to enter into the market and gain the early-comer advantages in this lucrative industry with hundreds of billions dollar potentials.

(1) Some Advantages Taken by Internet Giants

One of the advantages possessed by the e-trading platforms of JD, Taobao and Suning may lie in the e-business itself. As a subsidiary of these e-business firms, the equity crowdfunding platforms have an easy access to large number of e-business participants and huge internet traffic. Many equity crowdfunding participants were already educated and cultivated by these internet giants earlier through the reward crowdfunding that were conducted by these internet giants earlier. Therefore, it was much easier for the platforms to add or convert these reward crowdfunding investors to the list of the equity crowdfunding investors. On the other hand, from the investor perspective, the reputation and popularity accumulated by these giants' reward crowdfunding platforms also made the equity crowdfunding projects attractive as the trust-worthy investment targets for the these investors.

Another advantage of crowdfunding model, including both equity and reward types, taken by these internet giants is the extra role of the crowdfunding that is played as a market testing tool. The response from the investors can be used as a real time verification of the market demand and the popularity of the proposed projects or products, which will be a very important guidance for the platforms and leading investors in screening equity crowdfunding projects later on.

On the other hand, the advantage of Baidu and Qihoo 360 lies in their search engines. The traffic and the degree of attention carried by the platforms are very crucial for the promotion and development of equity crowdfunding platforms in the early stage.

(2) Some Features of the Leading Internet Firms' Platforms

All these leading internet giants possess abundant resources in the various areas of their businesses. They can relatively easily convert their customers in other business lines to be the customers of their equity crowdfunding platforms. As a result, they built up their own financial ecosystem, where their equity crowdfunding business line and other business lines can mutually support each other. More specifically, each leading internet firm's platform reveals some specific features in their business build-up as follows.

1. **Antsdaq:** Three Layers of Investors

Antsdaq of Alibaba set up three layers of investors in its equity crowdfunding business. The first layer of investors are these strategic investors, who can bring in some "strategic" resources or partners for the development of the platform, such as marketing partners and celebrity spokesperson.

The second layer of investors are called financial investors, who are typically the venture capitalists or other professional institutional investors or individuals that can help the platform raise needed funds during its development, such as VC and angel investors.

The third layer of investors are "user investors". These investors are also the long-term loyal customers or users of the firm's products, who are confident in the firm's future and willing to take shares of the firm's equity. As a result, they play a double role in Antsdaq's business as both customers and investors.

2. **JD Dongjia:** A Crowd Innovating Ecosystem

By integrating the existing JD entities, JD Dongjia created a comprehensive crowd-innovation ecosystem, covering the JD's primary business lines, such as JD Finance, JD Daojia (a delivery service), JD Mall (the primary trading or market place), JD's investment arms such as JD Crowd-Innovation Fund and Eyas Plan, JD's supply chain services such as Fund-Raisers Alliance and B2B Platform, and JD's training facilities such as JD Crowd-Innovation College and Small Class, and formed a one-stop-shopping service platform for entrepreneurship and innovation.

3. **Suning Private Equity Financing:** Entrepreneur Camp

Targeting the college students and young entrepreneur group, Suning raised capital to establish a venture capital fund of RMB 30 million to support the setup of the "Entrepreneur Camp", which provides a comprehensive entrepreneurial incubation services including funds, facilities, training, marketing promotion, and product sales.

4. **Baidu Baizhong:** Baidu Ecosystem

Baidu utilized its rich resources to provide the start-ups with financing service and other services across the full life cycle of an enterprise, such as brand promotion through Baidu Search and Baidu Poster, technical support through Baidu Open Cloud and Baidu Big Data, and channel services through Baidu Sticky Rise and Baidu Map.

5. **360 Gold Wash:** "Future Pricing"

360 cooperated with some leading investment institutions to screen out some projects that already received their A-round investment, and then, sign an investment and financing agreement. 360 will first transfer the funds raised through equity crowdfunding to these post-screen companies for their daily operations. Once these firms obtain the equity funds of next round within the pre-specified period of time, the crowdfunding funds will be converted into shares with a discount according to

new valuations. If the firms fail to obtain the next round of financing within the pre-specified period of time, the crowdfunding funds will be converted into shares according to the valuations of the last round.

(3) Threshold for Investors

Equity crowdfunding investors, as mentioned earlier, are generally classified into leading investors and following investors. The threshold for leading investors is usually higher with more constraint qualification requirements, such as angle investors with successful exit experiences, or institutional investors with leading investment experience or successful entrepreneurial experiences. In comparison, the threshold for following investors is more flexible, such as high annual income (RMB 300,000 in the recent years); or more than RMB 1 million personal financial assets, which include bank deposit, stock, bond, fund shares, assets management plan, bank wealth management products, trust plan, insurance products and future products; or professional investors who, at least, once worked in professional financial institutions.

It seems that the thresholds set up by the above five leading internet firms are basically similar, and only the requirements of Suning Private Equity Financing are slightly higher (Table 3.3).

(4) Legal Restrictions on Equity Crowdfunding

As the equity crowdfunding involves in equity investment, the current laws and regulations on equity investment also impose the restrictions on equity crowdfunding. The related laws and regulations can be summarized as follows:

Company Law—"A limited liability company shall be established by no more than 50 shareholders; For the establishment of a stock shareholder owned company, there shall be more than two but less than 200 initial investors."[10]
Securities Law—"Raising funds only from the specific investors of no more than 200."[11]
Partnership Law—"A limited partnership shall be established by more than two but less than fifty partners."[12]

The Tentative Measures for Management of Private Equity Financing (Draft)—"The standard of the qualified investors for private equity financing is no less than RMB 3 million of personal financial assets or the average annual income of the most recent three years no less than RMB 500,000. The number of shareholders of the fundraising firm should be no more than 200."[13]

The laws and regulations imposed strict restrictions on the number of investors in equity crowdfunding. As a result, the project initiators and platforms have the

[10]http://www.npc.gov.cn/wxzl/gongbao/2014-03/21/content_1867695.htm.
[11]http://www.npc.gov.cn/npc/lfzt/rlyw/2015-04/23/content_1934291.htm.
[12]http://www.gov.cn/flfg/2006-08/28/content_371399.htm.
[13]http://www.sac.net.cn/tzgg/201412/t20141218_113326.html.

Table 3.3 Threshold of following investors of five leading internet companies

Platform	Threshold of following investors
Suning Private Equity Financing	Qualified individual investors shall meet any of the following conditions: (1) Personal financial assets shall exceed RMB 3 million (2) Personal average annual income of the recent three years shall not be less than RMB 500,000 (3) The minimum amount invested in a single financing project shall not be less than RMB 1 million (4) Other investor requirement s as specified in relevant laws and regulations
Baidu Baizhong	Qualified individual investors shall meet any of the following conditions: (1) Personal average annual income of the recent three years shall not be less than RMB 300,000 (2) The financial assets shall not be less than RMB 1 million (3) Professional investment institutions/personnel
360 Taojin	Qualified individual investors shall meet any of the following conditions: (1) Personal average annual income of the recent three years shall not be less than RMB 300,000 (2) The financial assets shall not be less than RMB 1 million (3) The investors once worked in professional investment institutions
Antsdaq	Qualified individual investors shall meet any of the following conditions: (1) Individuals whose average annual income of the recent three years is not less than RMB 300,000 (2) Individuals whose financial assets are not less than RMB 1 million (3) Other individuals meeting the investment requirements for qualified investors
JD Dongjia	Qualified individual investors shall meet any of the following conditions: (1) Personal average annual income of the recent three years shall not be less than RMB 300,000 (2) The financial assets shall not be less than RMB 1 million

Data Source www.yingcanzixun.com

need to find some senior investors with rich resources, who can truly help the companies grow, within the limited number of investors under the cap.

At present, there are two primary ways to solve the issues of limited number of shareholders in China's equity crowdfunding:

(1) Entrusting Shareholding: A shareholder who registered with his/her real name can sign an entrusting-shareholding agreement with several or even dozens of equity crowdfunding shareholders whose names will not appear on the registration, respectively, and will represent these anonymous equity crowdfunding shareholders to hold their respective shares of fundraising company, as the Judicial Interpretation to the Company Law promulgated by the Supreme People's Court recognized the legitimacy of entrusting shareholding. Under this

arrangement, many equity crowdfunding shareholders do not hold shares directly by themselves, instead, their shares will be held by only one shareholder with real name in registration, and only this person's identity appears on the industrial and commercial registration. As a result, more actual investors than what the cap allowed can legally participate in equity crowdfunding.

(2) Platforms Holding: Under the platform-holding model, a share-holding platform can be first set up by, say, fifty equity crowdfunding shareholders; then, the share-holding platform can invest the funds that were raised through equity crowdfunding. In this case, the share-holding platform, instead of the fifty original investors, will serve as the shareholder of the fundraising company. So the number of the actual investors can legally go beyond the cap that is set up by laws.

3.3 Charity Crowdfunding

3.3.1 The Current Status of Charity Crowdfunding in China

On March 16, 2016, the Fourth National People's Congress Standing Committee held its plenary meeting, and the Charity Law of People's Republic of China[14] was passed, effective from September 1, 2016. The Article 31 of the Charity Law specifies that: Any organization or individual without the qualifications for public fundraising shall not be allowed to raise funds through public fundraising, but allowed to cooperate with the charity organizations with such qualification to conduct public fundraising; and the raised funds shall be managed by the charity organizations with the qualification for public fundraising. In particular, individuals cannot raise funds publicly, but are allowed to seek help from the qualified entities.

On August 22, 2016, the portal website of China's Ministry of Civil Affairs released an announcement with the list of the first group of internet fundraising information platforms of charity organizations. The announcement showed that the Ministry of Civil Affairs reviewed totally 29 internet fundraising information platforms for a format examination, and approved 13 platforms as the first group of internet fundraising information platforms of charity organizations, including Taobao Charity Internet Fundraising Information Platform and JD Charity Internet Fundraising Information Platform (Table 3.4).

According to a quarterly statistics of Yingcanzixun, by the end of September 2016, there were 49 crowdfunding platforms involved in charity crowdfunding in total. Among them, there were as many as 36 comprehensive platforms with charity crowdfunding projects, and there were only 13 vertical charity crowdfunding

[14]Portal website of the central government: Charity Law of People's Republic of China (Presidential Decree No. 43). March 09, 2016, http://www.gov.cn/zhengce/2016-03/19/content_5055467.htm.

Table 3.4 The list of 13 internet fundraising information platforms of charity organizations

Platform name	Entity name
Tencent Charity Online Fundraising Platform	Tencent Charity Foundation
Taobao Charity	Zhejiang Taobao Co., Ltd.
Ant Group Charity Platform	Zhejiang Ant Micro-and-small Financial Service Group Co., Ltd.
Sina Micro Charity	Beijing Weimeng Chuangke Network Science & Technology Co., Ltd.
China Charity Information Platform	China Charity Alliance
JD Charity Internet Fundraising Information Platform	China Bank Payments (Beijing) Science & Technology Co., Ltd.
China Foundation Center	Beijing Sijiu Non-profit Organization Development Research Center
Baidu Charity Information Center	Baidu Online Network Technology (Beijing) Co., Ltd.
Gongyibao	Beijing Hopu Juyi Technology Co., Ltd.
Xinhua Charity Service Platform	Xiahua Network Co., Ltd.
Fun in Funding	Beijing Fun in Funding Network Science & Technology Co., Ltd.
United	Shanghai United Foundation
Guangzhou Charity Information Platform	Guangzhou Charity Foundation

Data Source The Ministry of Civil Affairs of China

platforms. All these charity crowdfunding platforms are primarily located in 18 provinces and cities. Among them, Guangdong ranks the first with 12 platforms; followed by Shanghai with 11 platforms; Beijing ranks the third with 9 charity crowdfunding platforms; Jiangsu, Hebei and Liaoning co-rank the fourth with 2 platforms, respectively; and there is 1 platform in each the other 11 provinces and cities. The statistics showed that the charity crowdfunding in China is still in its early stage with the small scale, and only few platforms carry out the charity crowdfunding projects (Fig. 3.4).

3.3.2 The Procedures of Charity Crowdfunding

As a non-for-profit crowdfunding, the charity crowdfunding is more open and efficient in fundraising, compared with the traditional charity fundraising activities. The primary procedures of charity crowdfunding are as follows, and the charity crowdfunding platform of Tencent Lejuan is taken as an example:

1. The project initiators launch the projects, and fill the registration form with the information about the identity of the project initiators as either pubic fundraising institutions, or non-public fundraising institutions, or individuals. The platform

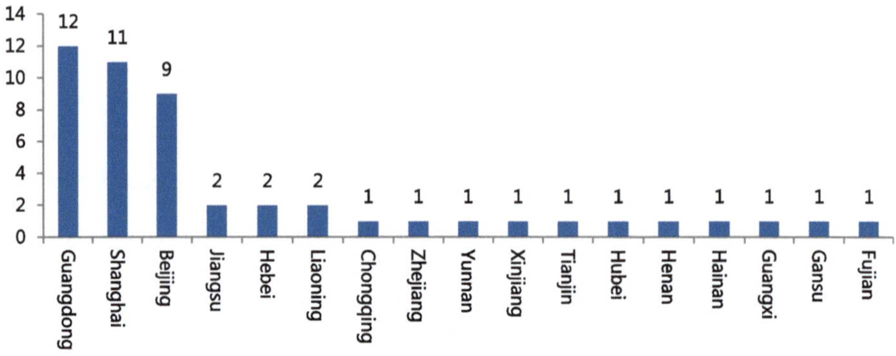

Fig. 3.4 Regional distribution of charity crowdfunding platforms. *Data Source* www.yingcanzixun.com

will review the form, and approve the application promptly after verification of the authentication. The applications submitted by public fundraising institutions and non-public fundraising institutions are usually reviewed within 5 business days.

2. The projects launched by public fundraising institutions can start fundraising directly after the web design and the posting content being confirmed by the platforms. For the projects launched by non-public fundraising institutions or individuals, however, the validity, design, and feasibility of the projects need to be first reviewed by public fundraising institutions, and the public fundraising institutions will suggest whether the projects should be supported.
3. Then, the fundraising begins. During the fundraising period of time, if the fundraising project starts its execution, the progress should be updated. For the projects launched by individuals and non-public fundraising institutions, after the funds being successfully raised through supporting public fundraising institutions, the project executors need to sign an agreement with the supporting public fundraising institutions. Upon receiving the agreement sent by the project executors, public fundraising institutions will transfer the funds to the project initiator's or executor's account within the pre-specified period of time. For example, Renren Charity Fund of China Foundation for Poverty Alleviation will transfer funds within 5 business days after receiving the agreement.
4. After fundraising target is reached, it will generally enters into the stage of project execution. The project executors will execute the project according to the published schedule, and update the progress in a timely manner.

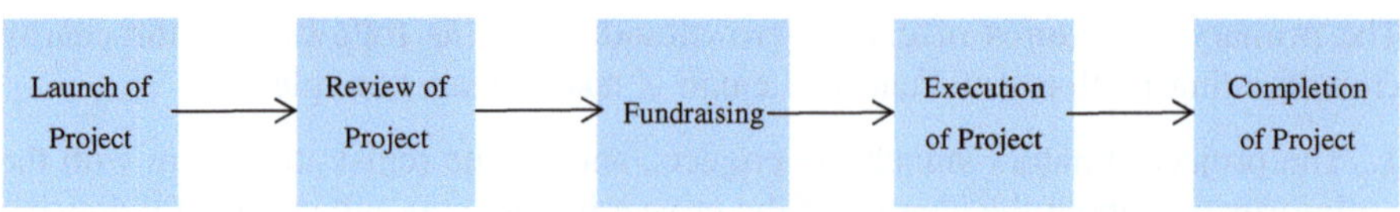

Fig. 3.5 The procedures of charity crowdfunding. *Data Source* www.yingcanzixun.com

5. After the financed project is completed, the project initiators, executors and public fundraising institutions are responsible for writing up a summary report, providing all the details of fund use and execution results to all investors. This process, in general, will be fully transparent to all investors (Fig. 3.5).

Chapter 4
Market Analysis of Sub-fields of Crowdfunding Industry

Zhi Chen and Haimei Wang

4.1 The Film, Television and Culture Crowdfunding

4.1.1 The Current Status of Film, Television, and Culture Market in China

(1) The Current Status of Theatre Movie Market

In recent years, with the improvement of living standard of consumers in China and the increased construction of movie theatre, film has become an integral component of the cultural life of general public. As a result, China's film market has been under a rapid development with box-office sales record being constantly renewed.

According to China's State Administration of Press, Publication, Radio, Film and Television and the General Office of State Commission for Management of Special Fund on Film Development (hereinafter referred to as the General Office), there were 1.057 billion viewers watching movie between January and September 2016, which is equivalent to 3.8577 million people watching movie every day. During the same period of time, the national box-office sales exceeded RMB 35 billion, increasing by 7.4% compared with RMB 33.009 billion between January 2015 and September 2015. The 9-month number of 2016 reached 80.43% of the total box-office sales of the entire year 2015, exceeded the annual box-office sales of 2013, and was about 2.08 times higher than that of 2012 (Fig. 4.1).

Z. Chen (✉) · H. Wang
Shanghai Wenxi Investment Consulting Co., Shanghai, China
e-mail: chenzhi@wdzj.com

J.G. Wang et al. (eds.), *Financing from Masses*,
https://doi.org/10.1007/978-981-10-5843-1_4

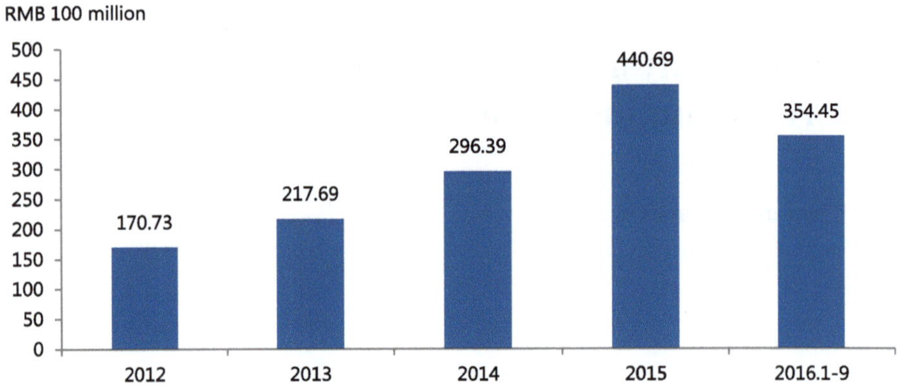

Fig. 4.1 Total box-office sales in China: 2012 to September 2016. *Data Source* China's State Administration of Press, Publication, Radio, Film and Television and the General Office of State Commission for Management of Special Fund on Film Development, www.yingcanzixun.com

(2) The Current Status of Online Film and Television Market

As the internet and mobile end equipment developed rapidly in the recent years, online mini movie, online movie or "big movie", online drama, and online entertainment also grew in a fast pace. As online movie and online drama do not need to wait for a long time for channel scheduling, as happened for the movies shown in theatres, and are not subject to the restrictions of governmental policies and regulations, the topics of these movies and dramas are more diverse, and these online programs are more popular among the younger audiences and grassroots directors, which triggered the emergence and mushroom of a large number of online movies and online dramas, such as Time Raiders, The Mystic Nine, and Remaining Crime. In addition, due to the lower threshold and lower cost, making online mini movie also became a notable way for many grassroots movie dreamers to realize their dreams. These short, concise and humorous stories were loved and supported by more and more netizens. Similarly, online entertainment also sprung up with its relaxing and funny style, as well as the humorous and real time topics. A large number of online entertainment programs emerged in the recent years with widespread attention from general public, such as Let's Talk, Are You Normal, and Intelligence Bureau on Mars.

Overall, with the rapid development of mobile internet technology, the popularity and penetration of internet is greatly increased. As a result, the number of online video users also grows at a faster pace, and more capitals and professionals flow into the industry of online video making, which lead the online film and television to become a flourished field with ever increased popularity and well diverse programs.

4.1.2 Some Backgrounds and Features of Film and TV Crowdfunding

(1) Some Backgrounds of the Film and TV Crowdfunding

In July 2011, the China's first domestic crowdfunding platform Demohour went online, which marks the inception of China's crowdfunding industry. As the rise and rapid development of the crowdfunding, the concept is quickly applied in various markets, including film and TV industry. With the great popularity of a domestic animation movie Monkey King: Hero is Back in 2015, the film and TV crowdfunding behind the movie also became known to more and more investors, and a wave of film and TV crowdfunding was sparked. The reasons behind the fast growth of the industry include three issues that exist in the film and TV market: difficulty in financing through conventional channels, higher enthusiasm towards film and TV by smaller investors, and the rise of internet entertainment.

A. **Difficulties in Financing Through Conventional Channels**

For making a movie, creative scripts, experienced directors, talent actors/actresses, and an effective production team are all important, however, the most critical issue is still financing. No matter it is in the pre-production stage or later promotion stage, a large amount of funds are needed. At present, the conventional ways of financing for entertainment companies primarily include joint production with multiple investors, PE/VC investment, bank loans, advertisement income by attached and embedded advertisement in the movies, pre-sales of copyright, and public listing. However, not all good movies can obtain adequate funds through these conventional channels, and it could be slow and bumpy even when the finance is available. It is particularly true for these teams with unknown younger members and the topics with small-sized audiences, to get favor through traditional financing channels. On the other hand, however, for the movies that only require median to low cost to produce, there are many potential smaller investors who have idle funds and are willing to invest. As a result, the film and TV crowdfunding were created and developed.

B. **The Enthusiasm of Small Investors**

Historically, film making has always been the privileges of large institutional investors and large entertainment media companies, due to the high investment threshold and strong technical focus, and it was not a game that allows the ordinary people to join and play. However, the emergence of film and TV crowdfunding opened the door for these smaller investors who are interested in investing in films and TV to participate. In particular, those films and TVs with strong sentiments, such as Big Fish and Begonia, could attract a lot of investors. By participating in film and TV crowdfunding, smaller investors can not only have the opportunity to enjoy investment earnings and peripheral products, but also the opportunity to receive some other non-monetary rights and benefits, such as visiting production team, recommending actor/actress, and taking photos with movie stars, which could strongly stimulate the enthusiasm of smaller investors.

C. **The Rise of Online Entertainment Products**

Year 2015 will be marked as the year of explosion of online drama and online movie. With the rapid growth of internet, the ever-improving functions of mobile terminal equipment, and the rise of the creation of literature works on internet, these original online dramas or films, which are either originally created or adapted from "internet literature" with novel subjects and style, are more and more favored by more and more audiences and fans. As mentioned earlier, it is always difficult for these types of dramas or movies to get financed from the traditional financing channels, and the emergence of crowdfunding provided them with a timely solution.

(2) The Characteristics of Film and TV Crowdfunding

As a new way of investment on the film and TV products, the film and TV crowdfunding revealed several distinct features, compared with the conventional financing models, as follows:

A. **Accessibility for Smaller Investors with Lower Threshold**

Compared with conventional financing channels, such as joint movie or TV making with multiple investors or PE/VC investment, the film and TV crowdfunding allows an incredible lower threshold with the minimum investment amount of only RMB 1 yuan, which enables a large number of smaller investors to participate. In addition, the low threshold is not only for investors, but also for project initiators. Any creative script can apply for crowdfunding without funding size restrictions. As a result, the film and TV crowdfunding not only satisfies the needs of smaller investors to participate in film and TV making, but also provides the younger and unknown movie directors with the opportunity of realizing their film making dreams.

B. **Diversified Ways of Returns**

Compared with the traditional ways of financing, the film and TV crowdfunding can provide more diversified ways of returns for investors, including both monetary earnings and non-monetary returns, such as visiting production team, taking photos with well-known movie stars, discussing film and TV making issues with directors, and even playing a role in the film or recommending actors/actresses. All these benefits will make the investment process more interesting for the smaller investors, and, in return, will attract more enthusiastic investors to participate.

C. **Promotion Effect**

As an investment with massive participation, the financing through the film and TV crowdfunding can generate enormous promotion effect in the market. When a movie or TV script raises funds through crowdfunding, which, in addition to the entertainment features of the film and TV products, may attract attention of general public, and the crowdfunding, or just the news of crowdfunding itself, can also attract attention from general public and produce strong promotional effect. As a recent example, Big Fish and Begonia, which was released in 2015, became a hot topic nationwide, not only because of its unique story of animation with a shooting period of 12 years, but also its way of financing through crowdfunding. Meanwhile, when large amount of smaller investors participated in film and TV crowdfunding, they will also promote these movies or TV series that they have invested through social medias before or after their release. For example, many investors made a block booking for the film Monkey King: Hero is Back last year.

4.1.3 Some Deeper Dive Analysis of the Film and TV Crowdfunding

(1) The Ways of Returns

As the film and TV crowdfunding raise funds through internet from mass investors with smaller investment size, the ways of providing returns for these smaller investors, as mentioned earlier, are also more diversified, including both monetary earning returns and non-monetary returns, or the combination of them.

- Monetary Earnings:
  The monetary earning type of returns primarily include returns with fixed return rate, returns with floating return rate, box-office sales returns, and equity returns. The sources of various returns are mainly coming from the profit sharing for online broadcasting, income from box-office sales, sales of copyright, and other incomes, such as these from embedded and attached advertisement. Among them, equity return is generally provided through transfer of part of equity of the film or TV products, which will eventually be offered in the form of shared income or distributed dividend.
- Non-Monetary Returns:
  Non-monetary returns usually take the form of reward crowdfunding, which primarily refers to the peripheral entertainment products, such as movie ticket and signature of movie stars.
- Other Forms of Returns:
  Other forms of returns primarily refers to some additional rights and benefits of investors, such as visiting production team site, playing a role in the movie or TV series, recommending actors/actresses, embedded advertisement, meeting and taking photos with well-known movie starts, and participating in some celebration events (Table 4.1).

According to a quarterly statistics of Yingcanzixun, by the end of September 2016, there were 1045 film and TV crowdfunding projects. Among them, 1029

Table 4.1 Various forms of returns

Types of returns	Forms
Physical rewards	Peripheral products, such as movie tickets, signed photos, posters and T-shirts
Monetary rewards	1. Fixed return rate 2. Floating return rate (A floating rate is presented according to the actual income of box-office sales or page view. For page view of 0–150 million clicks, the return rate is 10%; for page view of 150 million–200 million clicks, the return rate is 12%; and for page view more than 200 million clicks, the return rate is 14%) 3. Right of sharing profit or right to earnings (the income sources are generally the shared profit of online broadcasting, shared profit of box-office sales, advertisement income and copyright sales)
Beneficial rights	Visiting crews, playing a part, embedding advertisement, meeting and taking photos with stars and participating in celebration event

Data Source www.yingcanzixun.com

projects disclosed their ways of providing returns to investors, and the other 16 projects didn't release the related information.

Among the disclosed 1029 projects:

- The projects using the non-monetary returns ranks the first, with 273 projects;
- Followed by the projects using mixed return model of non-monetary returns plus other rights and benefits, with 256 projects;
- The projects adopting equity returns ranks the third, with 228 projects;
- Only 110 projects took the form of pure beneficial rights. The expected fundraising amount of this type of projects is usually small, and most of the projects are mini movies with low production cost;
- The projects adopting the mixed return model of equity earnings plus beneficial rights ranks the fifth, with 102 projects;
- There are 42 projects that took the mixed return model of non-monetary plus monetary returns;
- The projects used the mixed return model combining non-monetary return, equity earnings and beneficial rights comes last, with only 18 projects.

It seems that, at present, the primary way of providing returns for the investment through film and TV crowdfunding projects is non-monetary plus beneficial rights or plus monetary earnings (Fig. 4.2).

(2) Some Analysis of the Investment Fields of Film and TV Crowdfunding

There are several fields that attract film and TV crowdfunding in China so far, including primarily theatre movie, online movie, online drama, mini movie, TV play, entertainment programs, drama, documentary film, cartoon, and independent film making. Several metrics that can be used to assess the investment fields are as follows.

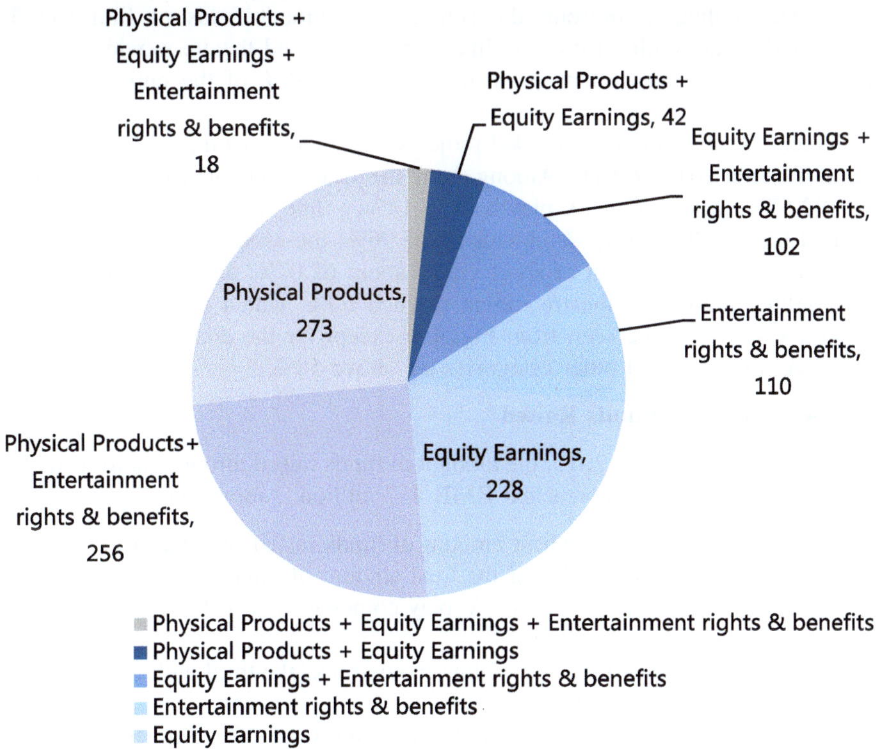

Fig. 4.2 Distribution of projects with different return models. *Data Source* www.yingcanzixun.com

1. **The Number of Successful Projects and Success Rate**

According to a quarterly statistics of Yingcanzixun, by the end of September 2016, the number of successful film and TV crowdfunding projects in China has reached 691. Among them,

- Most of the successful projects are online movie with 216 projects, accounting for 31.6% of the total number of successful film and TV crowdfunding projects in China;
- Online mini movie comes next with 160 successful projects, accounting for 23.15%;
- Drama ranks the third with 90 successful projects, accounting for 13.02%;
- Theatre movie ranks the fourth with 66 successful projects, accounting for 9.55%;
- Documentary film takes the fifth, with 41 successful projects; and
- The number of successful projects in the other six investment fields is between 4 and 40, respectively.

It appears that, at present, the primary investment fields of film and TV crowdfunding are online movie, online mini movie, and theatre movie, and together, their total successful projects account for 63.96% of the entire successful projects.

Percentage wise, there were 1043 projects with their investment fields disclosed, out of the total 1045 projects. Among them, the success rate of drama ranks the top with 82.57%; followed by TV play with 77.14%; online "big movie" ranks the third with 71.05%; followed by short video's 65.96%; the success rate of online mini movie is very close to that of short video, about 62.02%; and the success rate of both online drama and theatre movie reached 60%, which are 60.61 and 60%, respectively. As can be seen from Fig. 4.3, except for the entertainment projects, the success rates for all other categories are above 50%.

2. **The Amount of Funds Raised**

By the end of September 2016, the amount of funds raised through nationwide film and TV crowdfunding has reached RMB 417 million. Among them,

- Theatre movie has the highest amount of funds raised of RMB 150.0286 million, accounting for 36.02% of the total amount of funds successfully raised;
- The amount of funds raised by TV play comes next with RMB 112.5942 million, accounting for 27.03%;
- The amount of funds raised by online movie ranks the third with RMB 82.7764 million, accounting for 19.87%;
- Online drama ranks the fourth, and drama ranks the fifth, with the amount of funds raised up to RMB 46.8096 million and RMB 10.7267 million, respectively;

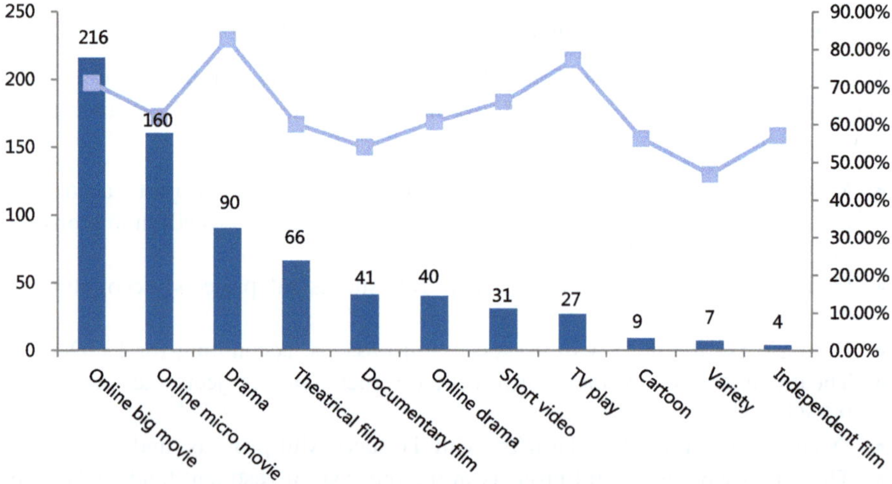

Fig. 4.3 The number of projects with successful crowdfunding and success rates. *Data Source* www.yingcanzixun.com

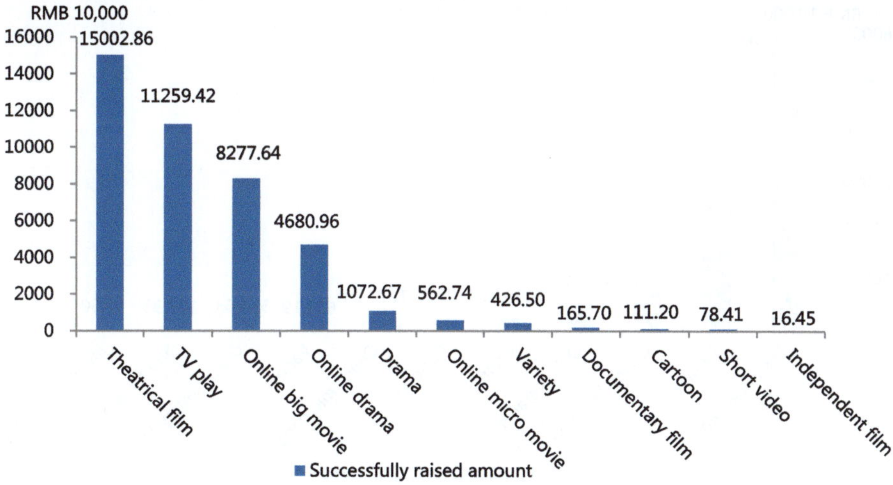

Fig. 4.4 Funds raised by various investment fields. *Data Source* www.yingcanzixun.com

- The amount of funds raised by online mini movie ranks the sixth with RMB 5.6274 million, accounting for 1.35%.

As can be seen from the data, online mini movie has the lowest amount of funds raised due to its low production cost, even though it has the largest number of successful fundraising projects. In general, the project initiators of the online mini movie set up a relatively low target for the amount of fundraising (Fig. 4.4).

3. **The Target of Fundraising Amount**

By the end of September 2016, the target of fundraising amount by nationwide film and TV crowdfunding has exceeded RMB 1 billion (RMB 1.02 billion, to be precise), and the target of fundraising amount of the projects that indicated their investment fields is RMB 999 million. Among them,

- The target of fundraising amount of theatre movies is the highest, up to RMB 560.5325 million;
- The target of fundraising amount of TV play comes next, with RMB 187.5991 million;
- Followed by the amount of online movie of RMB 139.7108 million;
- Online drama ranks the fourth, and drama ranks the fifth, with the targets of fundraising amount of RMB 46.4146 million and RMB 20.9631 million, respectively.

The target of fundraising amount for each of theatre movie, TV play and online movie is over RMB 100 million. Together, the total target of fundraising amount from these three fields accounts for nearly 90% of the total fundraising amount of film and TV crowdfunding. The higher target of fundraising amount of these fields reflect the high shooting cost in these areas (Fig. 4.5).

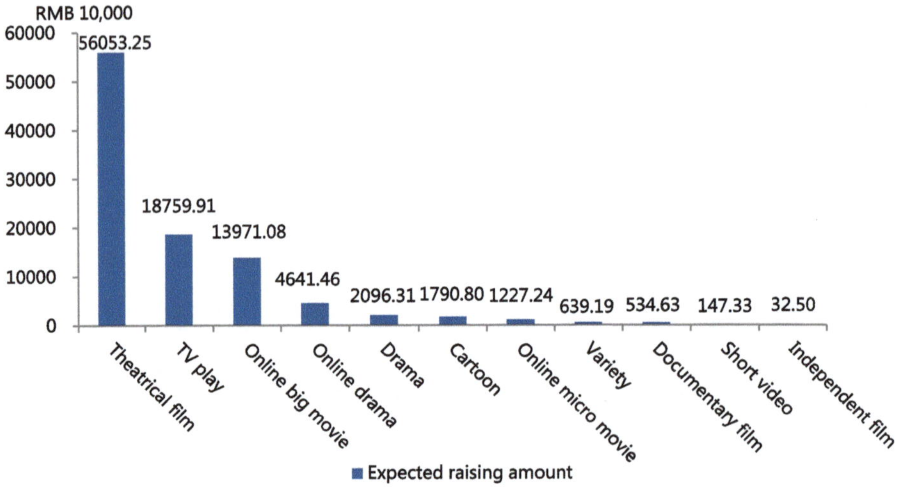

Fig. 4.5 The target fundraising amount in various fields. *Data Source* www.yingcanzixun

4. **The Number of Investors with Successful Investment**

According to a quarterly statistics by Yingcanzixun, by the end of September 2016, 145,200 investors have invested successfully in the film and TV crowdfunding industry in China, which doesn't include the projects with successful fundraising but not publishing the number of investors. Among these investors and their invested fields,

- Theatre movie ranks the top with 73,487 investors, accounting for 50.61% of the total successful investors of film and TV crowdfunding in China;
- Online movie comes next with 20,735 successful investors, accounting for 14.28%;
- Online mini movie ranks the third with 15,063 successful investors, accounting for 10.37%;
- Drama ranks the fourth, and online drama ranks the fifth with 11,128 and 6495 successful investors, accounting for 7.66 and 4.47%, respectively.

It appears that investors are most enthusiastic about theatre movies, which could be driven by the "movie star effect" and variety of ways of returns that theatre movie crowdfunding can provide (Fig. 4.6).

(3) The Distribution of the Target of Fundraising Amount

The target of fundraising amount of 1045 film and TV crowdfunding projects can be divided into five categories:

- The number of projects with the target of fundraising amount between RMB 100,000 (including RMB 100,000) and RMB 1 million ranks the top with 364 projects, accounting for 34.83% of the total number of projects;

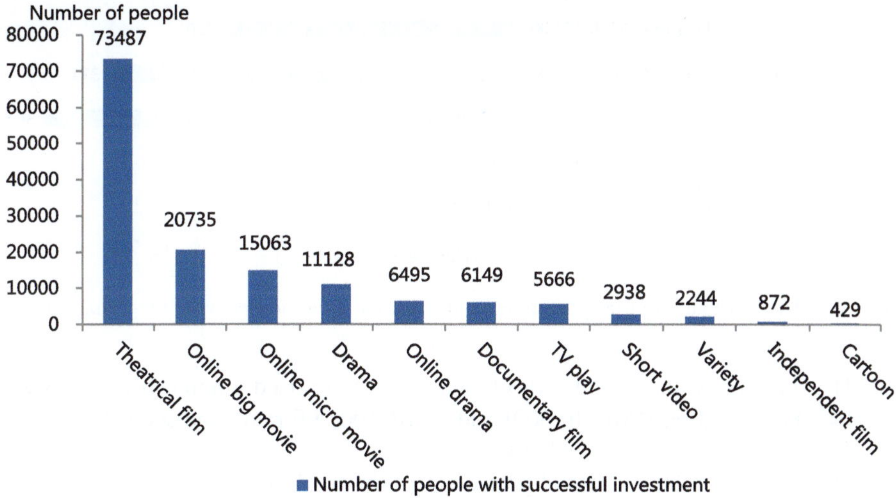

Fig. 4.6 Number of investors with successful investment in various fields. *Data Source* www.yingcanzixun.com

- The number of projects with the target of fundraising amount between RMB 10,000 (including RMB 10,000) and RMB 100,000 ranks the second with 311 projects, accounting for 29.6%;
- The number of projects with the target of fundraising amount below RMB 10,000 ranks the third with 220 projects, accounting for 21.05%;
- The number of projects with the target of fundraising amount between RMB 1 million (including RMB 1 million) and RMB 10 million ranks the fourth with 128 projects; and
- The number of projects with the target of fundraising amount above RMB 10 million is the smallest with only 22 projects.

It seems that the most film and TV crowdfunding projects are medium-and-small-sized projects. About 50.81% of the film and TV crowdfunding projects are with the target of fundraising amount below RMB 100,000, and 85.65% of projects with the target below RMB 1 million, while the projects with target of fundraising amount above RMB 1 million took a relatively small percentage (Fig. 4.7).

(4) The Distribution of Fundraising Amount of Successful Projects

The fundraising amount of 691 successful film and TV crowdfunding projects can be divided into five categories:

- There are 244 successful projects with the fund-raised amount between RMB 100,000 (including RMB 100,000) and RMB 1 million, which ranks the top, and accounts for 35.31% of the total number of successful projects;

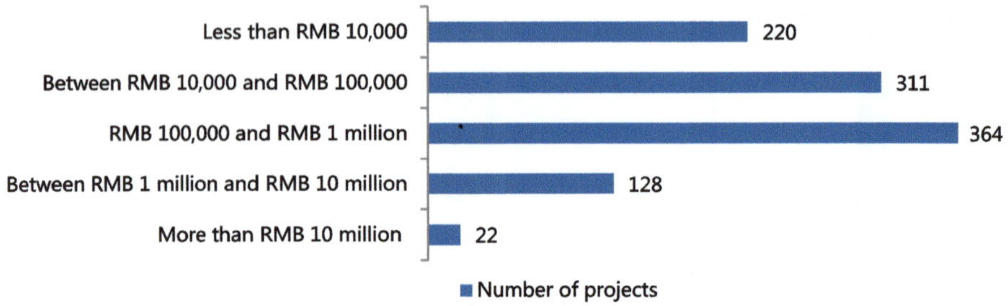

Fig. 4.7 The distribution of target of fundraising amount. *Data Source* www.yingcanzixun.com

- The number of successful projects with the fund-raised amount between RMB 10,000 (including RMB 10,000) and RMB 100,000 ranks the second with 197 projects, accounting for 28.51%;
- The number of the successful projects with the fund-raised amount below RMB 10,000 ranks the third with 153 projects, accounting for 22.14%;
- The number of the successful projects with the fund-raised amount between RMB 1 million (including RMB 1 million) and RMB 10 million ranks the fourth with 91 projects, accounting for 13.17%; and
- The number of the successful projects with the raised amount above RMB 10 million is the least, with only 6 projects.

Therefore, the most successful film and TV crowdfunding projects have the fund-raised amount below RMB 1 million, and, among them, the majority of the projects have the raised amount below RMB 100,000, with medium or low production cost (Fig. 4.8).

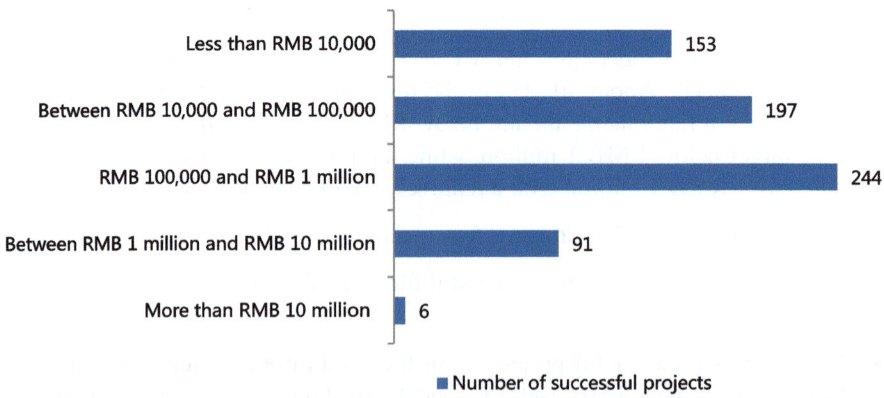

Fig. 4.8 The distribution of raised fund amount of successful projects. *Data Source* www.yingcanzixun.com

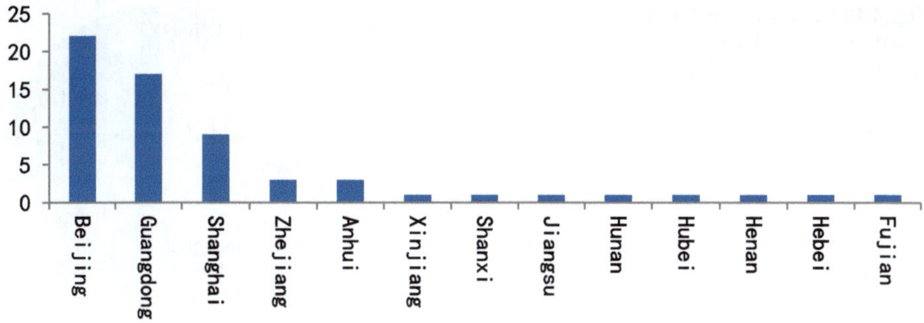

Fig. 4.9 Number of film and TV crowdfunding platforms by provinces. *Data Source* www.yingcanzixun.com

4.1.4 *Regional Distribution of Film and TV Crowdfunding Platforms*

(1) The Number of Film and TV Crowdfunding Platforms by Provinces

According to a quarterly statistics by yingcanzixun, by the end of September 2016, there were 62 film and TV crowdfunding platforms in China with normal operations. As mentioned earlier, most of them (37 platforms) are comprehensive film and TV crowdfunding platforms, and there were 25 vertical film and TV crowdfunding platforms. And all these crowdfunding platforms are located in 13 provinces and cities in China. As the birth places of the entire crowdfunding industry in China, Beijing and Guangdong host the largest number of film and TV crowdfunding platforms in China with obvious "centralization effect". As of the end of September 2016,

- Beijing continues to rank the top with 22 platforms;
- Guangdong ranks the second with 17 platforms;
- Shanghai ranks the third with 9 platforms;
- Zhejiang and Anhui co-rank the fourth, with 3 platforms, respectively;
- Each of the other 8 provinces (see Fig. 4.9 for the whole list) has 1 platform, respectively.

It can be seen that Beijing, Guangdong, Shanghai, Zhejiang and Anhui are the top five regions of China in terms of the number of film and TV crowdfunding platforms, accounting for 87.1% of the total number of nationwide platforms in China.

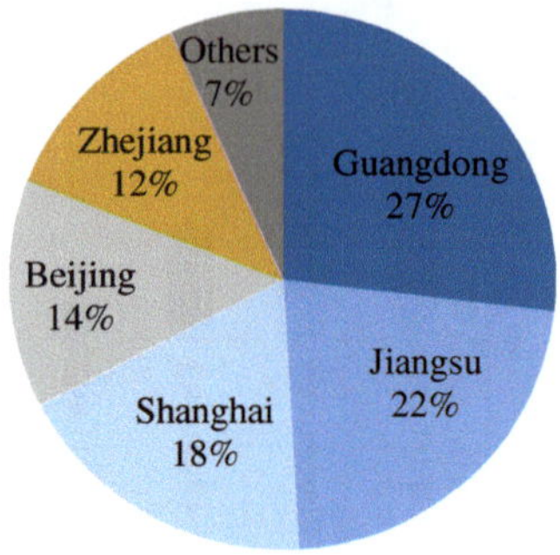

Fig. 4.10 The scale of funds raised by film and TV crowdfunding by provinces. *Data Source* www.yingcanzixun.com

(2) The Scale of Funds Raised by Provinces in China

By the end of September 2016,

- Guangdong, Jiangsu and Shanghai rank the top three for the scale of the funds raised, with the amount of RMB 111.8645 million, RMB 92.531 million, and RMB 76.0121 million, respectively;
- Beijing ranks the fourth, with the amount of funds raised up to RMB 51.0523 million;
- Zhejiang ranks the fifth, with the amount of funds raised up to RMB 51.0523 million.

The total amount of funds raised by the above five provinces and cities accounts for 93% of the total amount of funds raised by the entire country. These five provinces and cities undoubtedly take the leading position in film and TV crowdfunding, which is largely due to their well-developed economy and stronger investment consciousness with favorable policy support from local governments. Therefore, for the foreseeable short and medium terms, the crowdfunding scale in China will still be determined by these provinces and cities. In comparison, the other 23 provinces and cities with crowdfunding platforms, in total, only raised RMB 27.8795 million (Fig. 4.10).

4.1.5 The Success Rate of Film and TV Crowdfunding by Fields

As discussed earlier, theatre movie, online movie, and online mini movie take the lead in terms of the number of successful projects and the number of investors in the investment fields of film and TV crowdfunding. And some deeper dive analysis can be conducted as follows.

(1) The Success Rate of Theatre Movies

Among the successful theatrical movie projects:

- The number of the successful projects with the target of fundraising amount between RMB 1 million (including RMB 1 million) and RMB 10 million ranks the first, with 29 projects;
- The number of the successful projects with the target of fundraising amount between RMB 10,000 (including RMB 10,000) and RMB 100,000 ranks the second, with 15 projects;
- There are 12 successful projects with the target of fundraising amount between RMB 100,000 (including RMB 100,000) and RMB 1 million, ranking the third;
- There are 9 successful projects with the target of fundraising amount below RMB 10,000, ranking the fourth; and
- The number of successful projects with the target of fundraising amount above RMB 10 million is the least, with only 1 project.

In terms of the success rate of these theatre movie projects:

- The projects with the target of fundraising amount between RMB 10,000 (including RMB 10,000) and RMB 100,000 have the highest success rate, up to 83.33%;
- Followed by the projects with the target of fundraising amount below RMB 10,000, with the success rate of 81.82%;
- The projects with the target of fundraising amount between RMB 1 million (including RMB 1 million) and RMB 10 million have a success rate of 63.04%, whose return model is either equity returns or the combination of equity returns and other two forms of returns;
- The projects with the target of fundraising amount between RMB 100,000 (including RMB 100,000) and RMB 1 million have a success rate of 54.55%; and
- The projects with the target of fundraising amount above RMB 1 million (including RMB 1 million) have the lowest success rate of 7.69%.

As can be seen from the above data, the theatre movie projects with the target of fundraising amount below RMB 100,000 have the highest success rate, even though the number of the theatre movie projects with the target of fundraising amount above RMB 1 million are the majority. In this interval of the fundraising, the returns typically take the form of non-monetary or beneficial rights. With smaller investment amount, these projects are easier to attract and involve in the participation of investors (Fig. 4.11).

(2) The Success Rate of Online Movies

Among the successful projects of online movies:

- The number of the successful projects with the target of fundraising amount between RMB 100,000 (including RMB 100,000) and RMB 1 million ranks the first, with 178 projects;

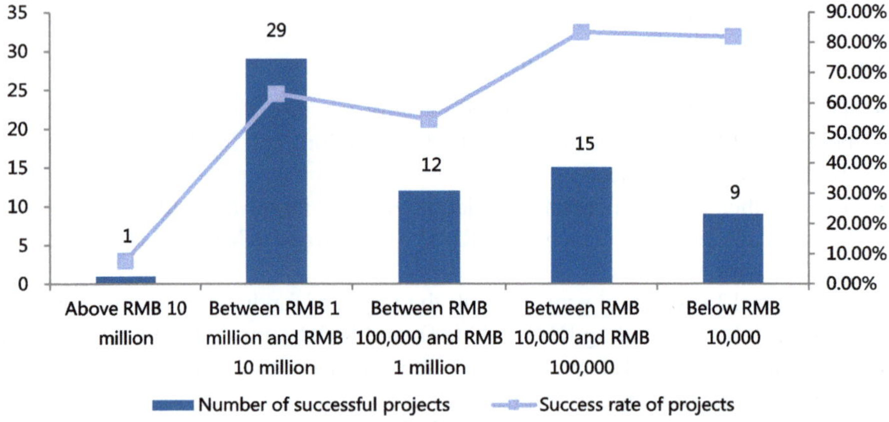

Fig. 4.11 The success rate of theatre movie projects. *Data Source* www.yingcanzixun.com

- The number of the successful projects with the target of fundraising amount between RMB 10,000 (including RMB 10,000) and RMB 100,000 ranks the second, with 20 projects;
- There are 16 successful projects with the target of fundraising amount between RMB 1 million (including RMB 1 million) and RMB 10 million;
- The number of the successful projects with the target of fundraising amount below RMB 10,000 is the least, with only 2 projects; and
- There is no project with the target of fundraising amount above RMB 10 million.

For the success rate of the online movie projects:

- The projects with the target of fundraising amount between RMB 100,000 (including RMB 100,000) and RMB 1 million have the highest success rate of 77.39%;
- Followed by the projects with the target of fundraising amount between RMB 10,000 (including RMB 10,000) and RMB 100,000, with the success rate of 64.52%;
- The projects with the target of fundraising amount below RMB 100,000 have a success rate of 50%; and
- The projects with the target of fundraising amount between RMB 1 million (including RMB 1 million) and RMB 10 million have the lowest success rate of 41.03%.

Therefore, the online movie projects with the target of fundraising amount between RMB 100,000 (including RMB 100,000) and RMB 1 million, and the equity return as the primary return form, appears to be the one that can more easily attract the participation of investors (Fig. 4.12).

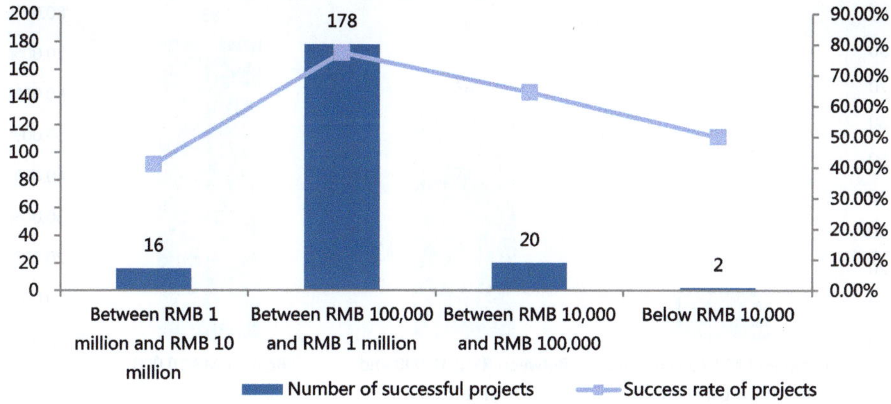

Fig. 4.12 The success rate of online movies. *Data Source* www.yingcanzixun.com

(3) The Success Rate of Online Mini Movies

Among the successful projects of online mini movies:

- The number of the successful projects with the target of fundraising amount below RMB 10,000 ranks the first, with 83 projects;
- The number of the successful projects with the target of fundraising amount between RMB 10,000 (including RMB 10,000) and RMB 100,000 ranks the second, with 63 projects;
- The number of the successful projects with the target of fundraising amount between RMB 100,000 (including RMB 100,000) and RMB 1 million is the least, with only 14 projects.

For the success rate of these projects:

- The projects with the target of fundraising amount below RMB 10,000 have the highest success rate of 71.55%;
- Followed by the projects with the target of fundraising amount between RMB 10,000 (including RMB 10,000) and RMB 100,000, with the success rate of 56.76%;
- The projects with the target of fundraising amount between RMB 100,000 (including RMB 100,000) and RMB 1 million have the lowest success rate, which is only 45.16%.

Therefore, the projects with the target of fundraising amount below RMB 10,000 have the highest success rate. Likely, the lower target of fundraising amount makes the objectives to be more easily achieved. However, the success rates of the projects in other two categories are also above 40%. The overall target of fundraising amount of online mini movie is below RMB 1 million, and the return model typically takes non-monetary return or beneficial rights (Fig. 4.13).

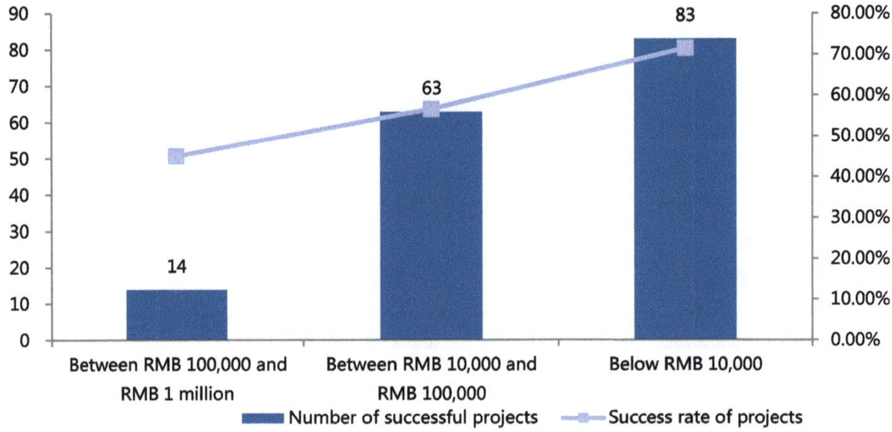

Fig. 4.13 The success rate of online mini movies. *Data Source* www.yingcanzixun.com

4.1.6 Financing of Vertical Film and TV Crowdfunding Platforms

According to a quarterly statistics of Yingcanzixun, by the end of September 2016, 3 vertical film and TV crowdfunding platforms obtained venture capital investment, including Kaipai, Taoyuji, and Yingdaren.

- Kaipai completed angel-round financing

Kaipai is a crowdfunding platform focusing on film industry, which raises funds for film products, especially for short videos, online movie and independent film. In November 2015, Kaipai obtained multiple million yuan of the angle-round financing, invested by Shenzhen Rongchuang Investments Co., Ltd.[1]

- Taoyuji received angel-round financing

Taoyuji (formerly known as Xingchou Net) is an internet crowdfunding platform specialized in the vertical sub-fields of entertainment industry. It started with online movie and went online in November 2015. As reported, Taoyuji has completed angel-round financing at the end of April 2016, with the funds invested by Suhehui.[2]

- Yingdaren obtained angel-round financing of RMB 2 million

Officially going online in December 2015, Yingdaren is a film and TV crowdfunding platform, starting with online movie, and providing equity returns for

[1]http://www.ocn.com.cn/news/touzi/201511/ewiqv12103330.shtml.

[2]http://www.toutiao.com/i6307356426775822849/.

Table 4.2 Financing of vertical film and TV crowdfunding platforms

Platform	Financing time	Round	Investor	Financing amount
Kaipai	In November 2015	Angle round	Shenzhen Rongchang Investments Co., Ltd.	Above RMB 1 million
Taoyuji (formerly known as Xingchou)	The end of April 2016	Angle round	Suhehui	RMB 4 million
Yingdaren	The end of May 2016	Angle round	Chuangmeng Investment	RMB 2 million

Data Source www.yingcanzixun.com

investors. At the end of May 2016, Yingdaren obtained the angel-round financing of RMB 2 million, invested by Mengchuang Investments (Table 4.2).[3]

4.1.7 The Risks of Film and TV Crowdfunding

In the past year, while the film and TV crowdfunding has been becoming increasingly popular in China, the risks that are inherited in the market also went with the growth of the industry. Some major risks associated with film and TV crowdfunding are identified as follows:

(1) Longer Investment Period

The making of film and TV requires a relatively longer shooting and production period of time. From selection of scripts, formation of the production team, shooting and production, and post-production review and approval by the State Administration of Radio Film and Television (SARFT), to setting up the schedule and going online, the entire process is long and complex. Most importantly, there is possibility that the movie or TV series under production may not be able to successfully pass the review of the SARFT, or couldn't be put on schedule for show at early times. For example, Big Fish and Begonia, which successfully obtained crowdfunding through Demohour in 2015, couldn't be scheduled and released in theaters until three years later after the completion of the movie production. In addition, part of returns for investors can only be received after film and TV products are released. As a result, it could take a long time for investors to obtain their returns.

[3]http://www.jiemian.com/article/691141.html.

(2) The Risks of Film and TV Investment

There is a high risk for investment in shooting film and TV products in China. Each year, there are many film and TV works are shot in the country, but only a few are eventually released, and very few can actually make profit. If taking film as an example, in the first half year of 2016, about 192 films are released, but the total box-office sales of top 15 films account for 70% of total box-office sales.[4] Therefore, a large part of box-office revenue is actually taken by only very few films with high box-office sales, and the profitability of the most released films is not impressive at all, if not mentioning that more films made even couldn't be released. As the final return of film and TV crowdfunding is directly linked to the box-office sales of films, and many uncertain factors such as viewers' preference, competitive films showed in the same period of time, film release time and scheduled show time may all influence the box-office sales, if the box-office sales of a film is not desirable, investors may not be able to get any returns, even could lose their principals.

(3) Imperfect Post-investment Management and Low Transparency

As a newly developed industry, the operation mechanism of film and TV crowdfunding platforms is far from perfect, and both pre-online review and post-investment management are less mature. There exist operational risk of lack of the due diligence by the platform, and the missing of the post-investment management, as well as the moral risk that either the platforms or/and the project initiators defraud. At present, many project initiators are not willing to actively disclose the project progress. As a result, the investors cannot gain the right of knowing the related information and are not informed for what happened for the financed project in a timely manner. In many occasions, for example, shooting budget could be listed very high, but only a small amount of money was indeed being used in actual shooting, and the investors know nothing about it.

(4) Insufficient Regulatory Policies

At present, the regulatory policies specifically related to crowdfunding have not been in place yet, but if the film and TV projects adopt the way of equity crowdfunding, they shall be subject to China's Securities Law, which limits the number of the accumulative participants of non-public issuance at no more than 200 investors. Therefore, there is a possibility for some film and TV crowdfunding platforms of conducting illegal fundraising activities for some equity type of projects. If that happened, due to insufficient regulations, investors' rights and benefits may not be effectively safeguarded.

[4]http://58921.com/alltime/2016.

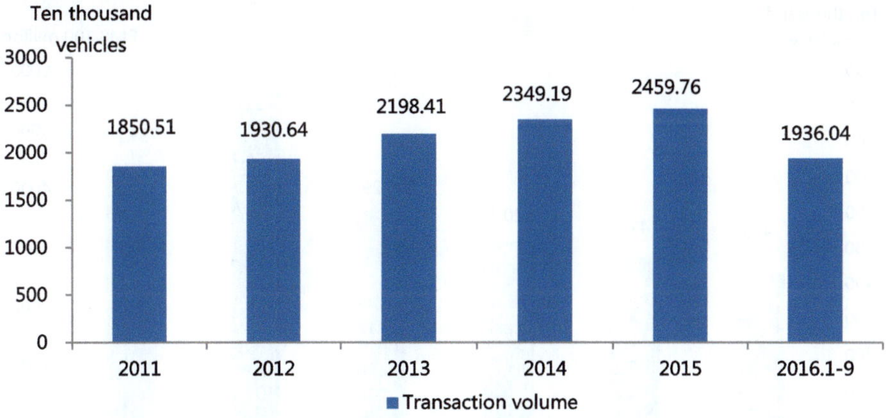

Fig. 4.14 New vehicle sales in China: 2011–September 2016. *Data Source* China Automotive Industry Association, www.yingcanzixun.com

4.2 Used Car Crowdfunding

4.2.1 The Current Status of Automobile Market in China

(1) The New Car Market

As the living standard in China continuously improves, automobile has become a major daily transportation tool for more and more commuters. According to the data released by China Automotive Industry Association, the volume of automobile sales from January 2016 to September 2016 was 19.3604 million, increasing by 13.17% on a 3-quarter (3Q)-over-3-quarter (3Q) basis, and reaching 78.71% of the annual volume sales of 2015.[5] For the past five years, as indicated in Figs. 4.14 and 4.15, the new automobile volume sales grew steadily, and its growth was far beyond the volume growth of the used-car market.

(2) The Used Car Market

In recent years, used car appears as a new choice of automobile buyers and has been favored by more and more consumers. According to the data released by China Automobile Dealers Association, 7.392 million used cars have been traded in China between January 2016 and September 2016, increasing by 7.37% on a 3Q-over-3Q basis, and up to 78.5% of the annual trading volume of 2015 and exceeding the annual trading scale of 2014. Between January 2016 and September 2016, the used

[5]China Automotive Industry Association: Basic Analysis of the Sales Status of Automobile Industry in September 2016, October 12, 2016, http://www.caam.org.cn/zhengche/20161012/1505199441.html.

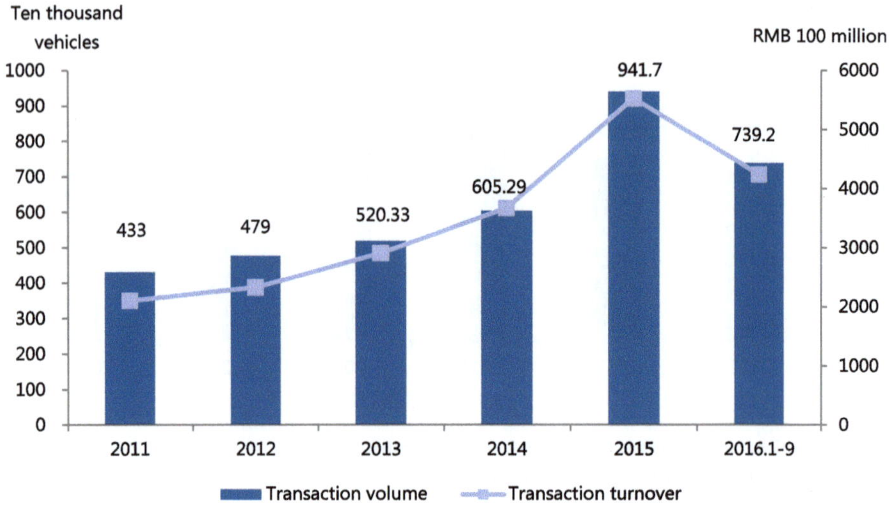

Fig. 4.15 Trading status of used car market in China: 2011–September 2016. *Data Source* China Automobile Dealers Association, www.yingcanzixun.com

car trading value of China has reached RMB 424.108 billion, which is about 76.67% of the total trading value of 2015. From the perspective of the trading volumes and trading values of used cars in the past five years, both the sales volumes and sales values of used cars grew rapidly, increasing by 56 and 51%, respectively, compared with 2015. However, China's domestic used car market is still in its early stage of development. Even though the sales volume and trading values are relatively stable in 2016, its growth potential is still tremendous.

4.2.2 Some Backgrounds and Characteristics of Automobile Crowdfunding

(1) The Background of Automobile Crowdfunding

1. **High Operating Cost of Traditional Used Car Dealers**

As it is usually observed, the traditional used car dealers in China often incur high operating cost, including labor cost, site rental, vehicle maintenance, as well as high commission paid to resale dealers, and are difficult to make profit if a used car stays in its storage for more than two months. As a result, used car dealers in China need to find other channels to more efficiently sell the used cars, and reduce the inventories.

2. **Difficulty in Financing**

The used cars are the key resource for used car dealers to run their businesses, and the used cars need to be purchased first by used car dealers before these used cars can be sold later to the ultimate consumers. Apparently, if the used car dealers only rely on their internal funding, the growth of their businesses will be severely hindered with shortage of funds. In China, however, it is not easy for these used car dealers to obtain loans from typically state-owned commercial banks, and it will take a long time to process the loan if granted. As a result, the used car dealers have to explore the alternative ways of financing. Luckily, there are many investors, at the same time, who have some idle funds in hand and look for investable opportunities.

3. **Transformation from P2P Online Lending Platforms**

Impacted by rectification of P2P online lending industry conducted by regulators in China in April 2016, and the implementation of some regulatory policies started on August 24, 2016, a large number of medium-and-small-sized P2P online lending platforms encountered increased difficulties for survival. Meanwhile, however, crowdfunding is still an area without regulations in place yet at moment, which may allow these medium-and-small-sized platforms to be able to survival, especially for these platforms that were previously engaged in vehicle lending business. As a result, many of them converted from P2P car loan lending platforms to automobile crowdfunding platforms.

4. **Favorable Government Policies in Automobile Industry**

In recent years, the central government in China has been taking a stance to encourage the development of automobile industry, especially for the used cars and the imported vehicles from small dealers, and issued several documents to promote the healthy development of the industry.

In July 2014, for example, the State Administration for Industry and Commerce issued the Announcement on Stopping Implementation of Filing for General Automobile Dealers and Authorized Brand Automobile Dealers.[6] The Announcement seized the requirement of filing at the Administration for general automobile dealers and authorized brand automobile dealers from October 1, 2014, which was widely considered a favorable step taken by the Administration to provide policy support for imported cars from other channels rather than general auto dealers.

On March 25, 2016, the General Office of the State Council issued "Opinions on Promoting the Convenient Transaction of Used Cars",[7] with eight rulings to stop

[6]State Administration for Industry and Commerce: Announcement on Stopping Implementation of Filing for General Automobile Dealers and Authorized Brand Automobile Dealers, GSSZI [2014] No. 145.

[7]General Office of the State Council: Some Opinions on Promoting the Convenient Transaction of Used Cars, GBF [2016] No. 14.

some existing practices that hinder the development of used car market, including that no new policies that could restrict the development of used cars market can be made, and the cancelation of the existing policies that restrict the used car market by the end of May 2016. Apparently, it is generally considered a good news for the used car market in China.

(2) Some Characteristics of Automobile Crowdfunding

1. **The Short Investment Time**

Compared with industries such as real estate, the turnover and "cash-out" of used cars are much faster and easier. Automobile crowdfunding platforms typically possess their own sales channels, which can help more quickly dispose the used cars with a relatively shorter period of time, and get the returns for investors, even though, there is still sluggish season from time to time for poor sales of the automobiles.

2. **Buy-back by Platforms**

Different from other types of crowdfunding, automobile crowdfunding platforms typically provide guarantee of buy-back from investors/sellers. That means that, if the vehicle listed on the platform for sale cannot be sold within the pre-specified period, the platforms or used-car dealers will purchase it at a price with premium. This buy-back guarantee provided by platforms certainly attracts the participation of investors/sellers.

3. **High Yields of the Investment**

The automobile crowdfunding can provide high yields for investors, which is highly correlated with the disposal time of the used cars. The yield typically takes the form of floating returns, and the disposal time after the successful crowdfunding directly determine the rate of returns. For example, if RMB 100,000 is the "crowd-funded" amount, and the sales price is RMB 105,000, then, if the vehicle is sold or disposed successfully on the same day when the crowdfunding successfully completed, the daily rate of return will be 5%, and the annualized yield will be as high as 1825%. Similarly, if the used car is disposed successfully on the 90th day, then the 3-month yield will be 5%, and the annualized yield will be 20%. Of course, the net return for the investors will be the above amount minus the returns paid to the platforms and used car dealers.

4.2.3 The Business Models and Legitimacy of Automobile Crowdfunding

Automobile crowdfunding is widely considered the most popular one of the year, with the bid-ask (offer) spread as the primary business model at present. According to the types of vehicles, the automobile crowdfunding can be generally divided into three categories: used car, imported car from channels other than general dealers or authorized brand car dealers, and new car, and the used car crowdfunding is the primary one. In addition, some crowdfunding platforms also conduct marketing, leasing, financial leasing, and disposal of cars with non-performing loans, but all these activities are very limited with small size or scale.

(1) The Bid-Ask Spread Model of Used Car Crowdfunding

The bid-ask spread model is the most popular one that is adopted in the used car crowdfunding at present. Under this model, the investors purchase vehicles through crowdfunding, and make profit through the price difference by consequently selling the vehicles. The operation procedures are as follows:

1. The used car dealers who plan to participate in crowdfunding submit applications to crowdfunding platforms;
2. The crowdfunding platforms review and evaluate project applications;
3. The projects will be posted online after passing evaluation, and the investors can choose and invest in the projects that they are interested in;
4. If crowdfunding succeeds, the platforms will purchase vehicles, transfer the ownership, and take the registration. In general, the platforms will sign an entrusting share-holding agreement with investors, and the platform staff will nominally hold the property right of the purchased used cars. If the crowdfunding fails, however, the already collected funds will be returned to the investors' account;
5. After purchasing vehicles, the platforms will usually store the vehicles in the used car dealers' shops, while they look for buyers;
6. If some interested buyers are found, the investors will vote to determine whether or not to sell the vehicles to these identified buyers. As usual, the rule of approval will be set up in advance, and 51% of positive votes will be required for approval. In addition, most platforms also set up a sales period, which is, in general, between 10 days and 90 days. If no suitable buyers, however, are found within the pre-specified period, most platforms or automobile dealers will purchase the used cars according to the price that is pre-agreed upon by all parties. In general, the price will contain a premium that is equivalent to an annualized rate of 8–18% over the crowdfunding price.
7. After the vehicles are sold out, the proceeds will be transferred to the platforms' account. The platforms will deduct the operating cost from the proceeds, and take out the platforms' commission, which is usually 30–50% of the premium. These commissions will be shared with the used car dealers, with the proportion that is pre-determined by the platforms and used car dealers. The rest of proceeds will be distributed to the investors according to the proportion of capital contributions of investors (Fig. 4.16).

(2) Crowdfunding of Imported Vehicle from Alternative Channels

The imported vehicles from alternative channels are the cars purchased by traders from overseas market, and brought into Chinese market for sales without the direct

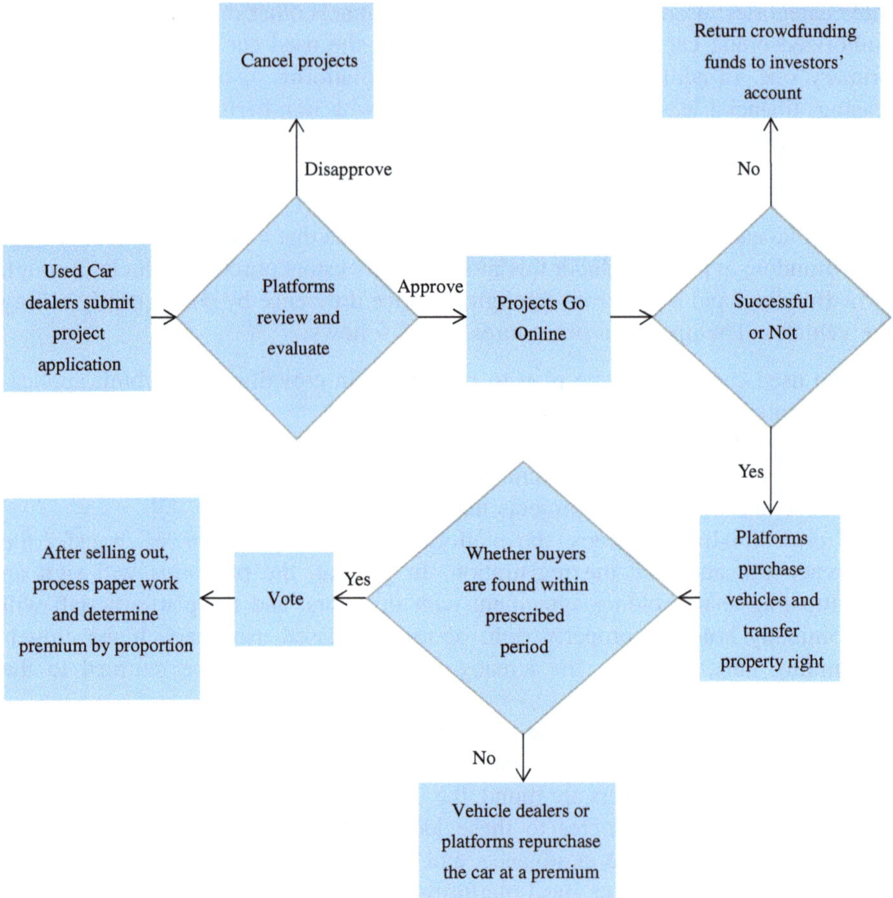

Fig. 4.16 Process of used car crowdfunding. *Data Source* www.yingcanzixun.com

authorization of brand manufacturers. According to the source difference, these imported vehicles can be classified into "American Cars", "Middle East Cars" and "Others", so they can be distinguished from the cars that are imported through authorized channels. As these imported vehicles from alternative channels skip the middle layers such as general dealers, regional dealers, and 4S stores, the sales cost could be significantly reduced. In addition, the dealers of these imported vehicle from alternative channels are not restricted by manufacturers' pricing policies, with much higher degree of freedom, so their selling price could be more preferential for buyers.

The crowdfunding of the imported vehicles from alternative channels also adopts the bid-ask spread model, and the operation procedures are basically the same with the used car crowdfunding. There is only one major difference in approval of selling. As discussed earlier, for the domestic used cars, the investors need to vote for approval of selling when a buyer is identified. In contrast, for crowdfunding of the imported vehicle from alternative channels, the investors do not need to vote to determine whether or not to sell vehicles. The imported vehicles will be directly sold at the sales price when any buyers would like to purchase it. Of course, if the vehicles fail to be sold out within the pre-specified sales period, then, the platforms or car dealers will purchase the car at a premium with the pre-agreed-upon annualized rate.

(3) The Legitimacy of Automobile Crowdfunding

As a newly emerged sub-industry, the rules and regulations in the automobile crowdfunding are not completely in place yet, which may bring in some legal risk for the operation of the automobile crowdfunding. For example, the electronic contract signed by investors specifies that the investors and the actual car holders who purchase the vehicles are referred to as "co-operators". They will contribute equity investment together to purchase the car, share the ownership of the purchased vehicles, and entrust the crowdfunding platforms to be the nominal registrant of vehicle at the registration agencies and hold the shares of the purchased vehicles.

According to the analysis by lawyers, however, there is no laws that prohibit entrusting holding of vehicles at present. As a result, as long as both parties signed an agreement and there is true automobile property, then, the entrusted holding of vehicles by platforms shall not be considered illegal. However, if the platforms commit to provide some types of returns on their marketing web page, even though it may not be included in the agreement, the commitment will still be regarded as a part of the agreement according to China's Advertisement Law. In this case, if the platforms promised to provide investment returns within certain period of time, and the platforms raise funds towards some non-targeted investors, then, the platforms may encounter the risk of illegal fundraising by the current laws and regulations in China. If the platforms committed to repurchase the car back at a premium within a pre-specified period of time conditionally, regardless whether or not the vehicles are sold out successfully, then, it could be considered as a lending activity by nature, then, subject to laws regulating debt financing, which may not be fully considered by the current transactions.

4.2.4 Some Statistics of Automobile Crowdfunding

(1) The Number of Automobile Crowdfunding Platforms in China

According to a quarterly statistics of Yingcanzixun, by the end of September 2016, there were 87 automobile crowdfunding platforms in China with normal operations, including 5 comprehensive automobile crowdfunding platforms, and 82 vertical automobile crowdfunding platforms, and it is expected that there will be more than 100 platforms in the entire year of 2016.

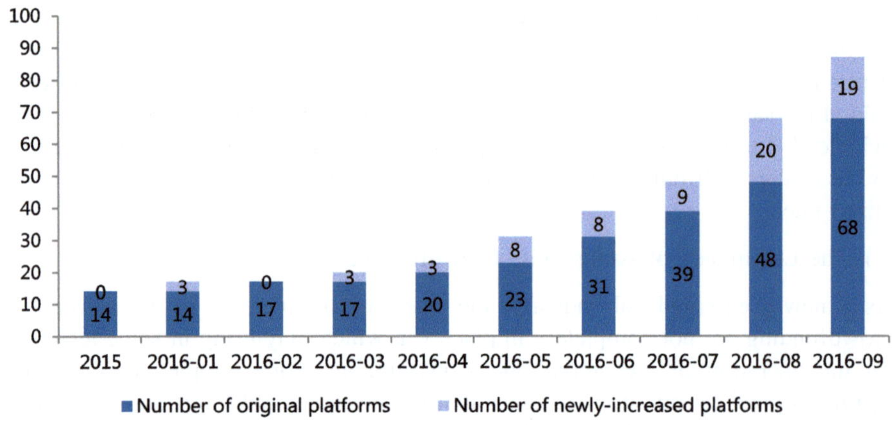

Fig. 4.17 Number of new automobile crowdfunding platforms: 2015 and 2016. *Data Source* www.yingcanzixun.com

For these newly established platforms, there were 73 automobile crowdfunding platforms that were set up in the first three quarters of 2016, about 5.21 times more than that of 2015. Among them, most of the new platforms, up to 48 platforms, appeared in the third quarter. As can be seen from Fig. 4.17 that there were new automobile crowdfunding platforms going online almost every month since January 2016. From May, however, the number of new platforms became sharply increasing, and reached the peak in August and September, with 20 and 19 new platforms, respectively. These time points well coincide the time period of rectification of P2P online lending industry in China, where the government regulators announced the rectification of P2P online lending industry in April and the policies were implemented in August. As a result of stricter regulations of P2P online lending field, many previous medium-and-small-sized P2P online lending platforms began to transform, and entered into the crowdfunding industry.

(2) The Number of Automobile Crowdfunding Platforms by Provinces in China

According to a quarterly statistics of Yingcanzixun, by the end of September 2016, the automobile crowdfunding platforms in China are located in 14 provinces and cities. Shandong ranks the top with a clear majority of 47 platforms; Jiangsu comes next, with 9 platforms; Guangdong and Hebei co-rank the third, with 5 platforms each; Shanghai and Anhui co-rank the fourth, with 4 platforms each. The number of platforms in Shandong accounts for 54% of the total number of automobile crowdfunding platforms in the whole country, which is largely due to the activeness of the used car market there. At the current stage, the automobile crowdfunding platforms primarily collaborate with used car dealers, and the transactions in the used car markets in several cities in Shandong, such as Zaozhuang, Linyi, and Jinan, are very active, and known as the three major national used car markets with large scale in China, which provided favorable market condition for the automobile crowdfunding (Fig. 4.18).

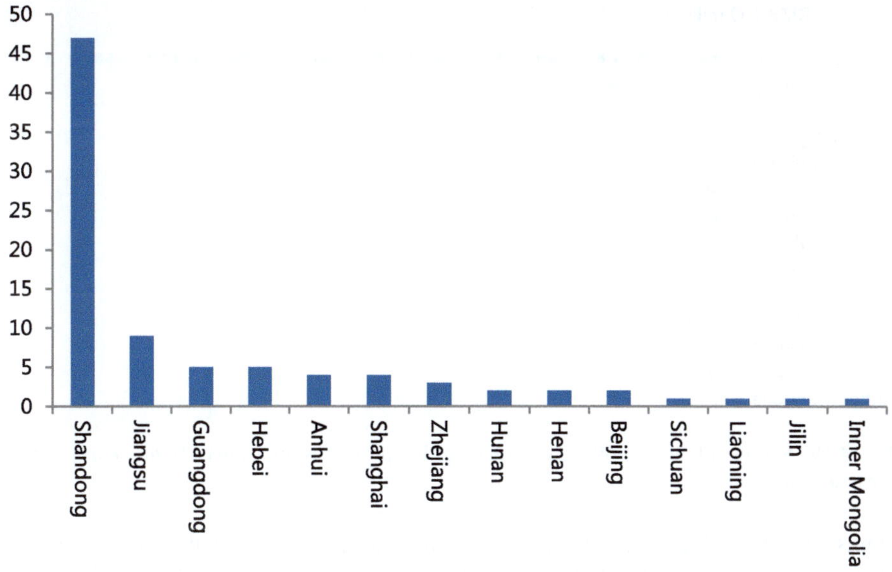

Fig. 4.18 Number of automobile crowdfunding platforms by provinces in China. *Data Source* www.yingcanzixun.com

(3) Successful Automobile Crowdfunding by Provinces in China

According to a quarterly statistics of Yingcanzixun, by the end of September 2016, RMB 6.313 billion has been raised by automobile crowdfunding platforms in China, and the total amount of the raised funds is expected to exceed RMB 8 billion by the end of 2016. Among the provinces and cities, Shandong ranks the top with RMB 3.514 billion; followed by Beijing, Jiangsu, and Guangdong, with RMB 1.269 billion, RMB 478 million, and RMB 457 million, respectively; the successfully raised funds through automobile crowdfunding in Zhejiang, Shanghai and Hebei are about RMB 150 million each; and the raised amount through automobile crowdfunding in other provinces, including Anhui, Sichuan and Hunan, is much less, which is no more than RMB 100 million (Fig. 4.19).

(4) The Number of Successful Automobile Crowdfunding Projects

According to a quarterly statistics provided by Yingcanzixun, by the end of September 2016, there were 14,173 successful automobile crowdfunding projects in China. Among them, the projects with the car sales price below RMB 200,000 ranks the top, with 4327 projects; the number of projects with the car sales price between RMB 200,000 and RMB 400,000 comes next, with 4070 projects. Apparently, the number of successful projects with the car sales price below RMB 400,000 exceeded 50% of the total number of the successful projects, and this price range appeared as the one that is most favored by investors. The number of projects with car sales price between RMB 400,000 and RMB 600,000 also went beyond 2000; and there were 1687 projects with sales price between RMB 600,000 and

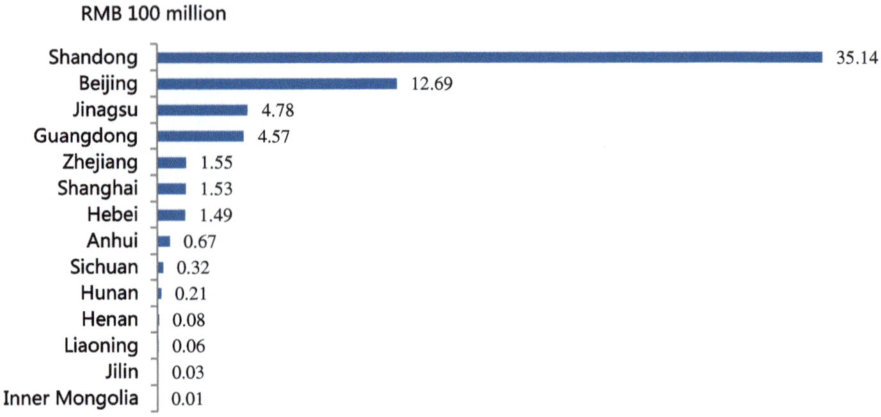

Fig. 4.19 Successful automobile crowdfunding by provinces in China. *Data Source* www.yingcanzixun.com

RMB 800,000. The projects (cars) with the car sales price in the range between RMB 800,000 and RMB 1 million and the interval between RMB 1 million and RMB 2 million are considered luxury cars, whose successful numbers are significantly less, with only 727 projects and 568 projects, respectively. Finally, the projects with car sales price above RMB 2 million are the ultra-luxury vehicles, with only 86 successful projects (Fig. 4.20).

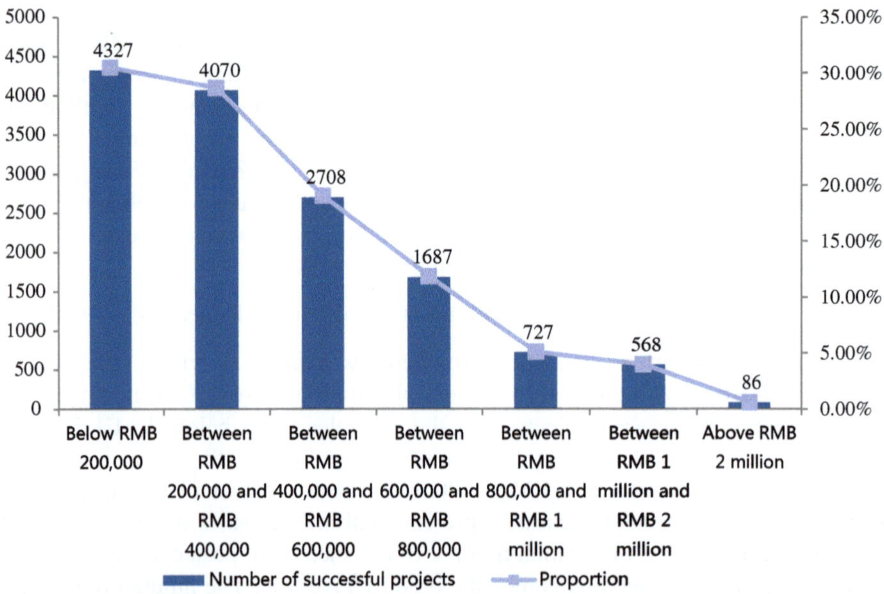

Fig. 4.20 Number of successful automobile crowdfunding projects by price range. *Data Source* www.yingcanzixun.com

4.2.5 *The Types and Brands of Automobiles Using Crowdfunding*

(1) The Number of Successful Automobile Crowdfunding Projects by Types of Cars

Among the 14,173 successful automobile crowdfunding projects in China, sedan ranks the top with 7862 cars, accounting for about 55.47% of the total number of the successful projects; SUV comes next with 5149 successful projects, accounting for 36.33%; sports car, minivans for commercial use, and pick-up truck rank the next, with about 100 projects each, but accounting for a very little percentage of the total number of the projects. In addition, there were 109 projects that deal with sales of trucks and limos (Fig. 4.21).

(2) The Raised Fund Amount of Automobile Crowdfunding by Types

In the total amount of RMB 6.313 billion that were successfully raised by automobile crowdfunding in China, the amount raised by sedan and SUV jointly accounts for nearly 90% of the total market, with RMB 2.967 billion and RMB 2.664 billion, respectively; and the amount raised by other types of vehicles only accounts for less than 10%: the sports car projects successfully raised RMB 506 million; and the scale of other types of vehicles including pick-up truck and minivan for commercial use is less than RMB 100 million (Fig. 4.22).

(3) The Investors and the Average Investment Amount of Car Crowdfunding by Types

According to a quarterly statistics of Yingcanzixun, by the end of September 2016, 360,400 investors have invested in automobile crowdfunding industry in China, with average investment amount up to RMB 17,500. The largest number of investors put their money in sedan projects, with nearly 180,000 investors; and the

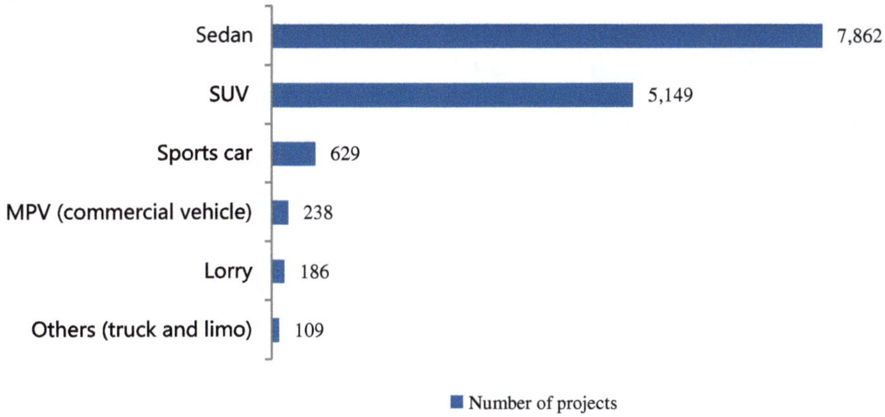

Fig. 4.21 Number of successful automobile crowdfunding projects by types. *Data Source* www.yingcanzixun.com

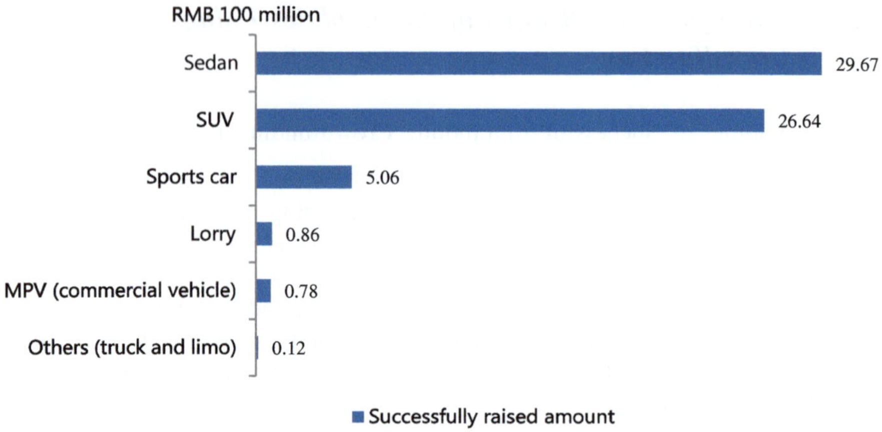

Fig. 4.22 Successfully raised amount of automobile crowdfunding by types. *Data Source* www.yingcanzixun.com

number of investors who invested in SUV projects ranks the second, with nearly 150,000 individuals; the numbers of investors who invested in sports car, pick-up truck, MPV and other types of vehicles are much less, with 24,300, 6700, 4400, and 600 investors, respectively. On the average investment amount, SUV, sports car, MPV and other types of vehicles, such as truck and limo, are far beyond the average level. The average investment amount of sports car is the highest, up to RMB 20,800; but the average investment amount of sedan and pick-up truck is lower than the average; and among them, the average investment amount of pick-up truck is the lowest, with only RMB 12,800 (Fig. 4.23).

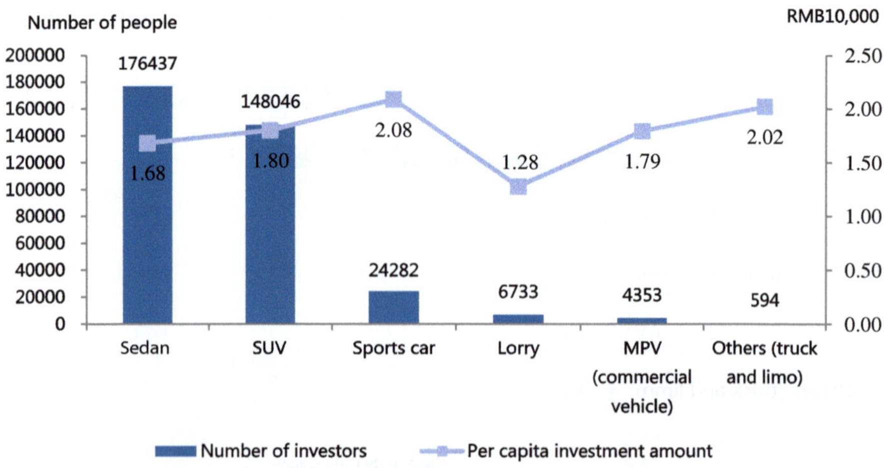

Fig. 4.23 Number of investors and average investment amount by types of cars. *Data Source* www.yingcanzixun.com

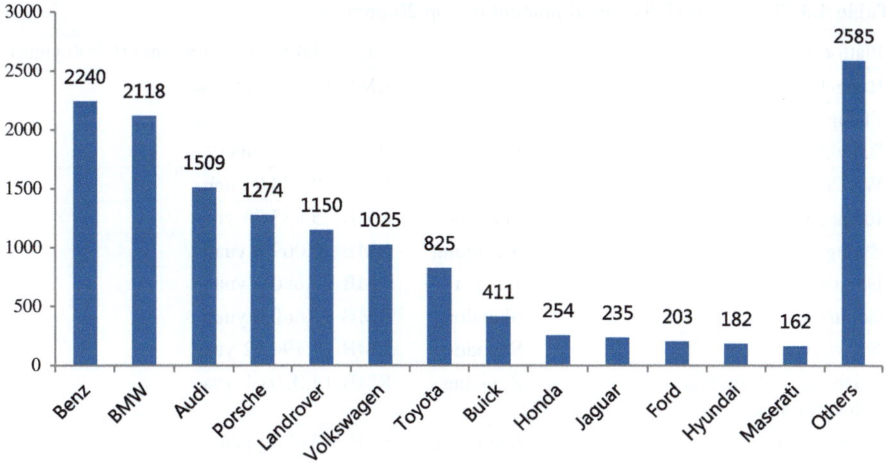

Fig. 4.24 Number of automobile crowdfunding by brands. *Data Source* www.yingcanzixun.com

(4) The Automobile Crowdfunding by Brand of Cars

By the end of September 2016, three Germany brands, Benz, BMW, and Audi rank the top three among all successful projects of automobile crowdfunding, with 2240 projects, 2118 projects, and 1509 projects, respectively; followed by Porsche and Landrover, with 1274 projects and 1150, projects respectively. Benz, BMW, Audi, Porsche and Landrover are the five most popular brands in automobile crowdfunding business; followed by Volkswagen and Toyota, with 1025 successful projects and 825 projects, respectively. In addition, Buick, Honda, Jaguar, Ford, Hyundai and Maserati also showed good performance. However, except for Buick, which had more than 400 successful projects, each of the other five brands had about 200 successful projects. Finally, other brands including Volvo, Kia, JEEP and Subaru had about 2585 successful projects in total (Fig. 4.24).

4.2.6 *Some Statistics of Automobile Crowdfunding Platforms*

According to a quarterly statistics of Yingcanzixun, by the end of September 2016, all automobile crowdfunding platforms that ranked on top 20 have successfully raised more than RMB 45 million, and 15 of them have cumulatively raised more than RMB 100 million. Among them, Rongche and eWealth rank the first and the second, with RMB 1.483 billion and RMB 1.32 billion, respectively; Baoyide ranks the third, with successfully raised amount up to RMB 556 million; WeiCi Finance ranks the fourth, with the accumulatively raised amount up to RMB 401 million; and Juchuang Crowdfunding ranks the fifth, with the accumulatively raised amount up to RMB 254 million. From regional perspective, 11 platforms among the top 20

Table 4.3 The successfully raised amount by top 20 projects

Platform	Region	Successfully raised amount (10,000 yuan)
Rongche	Shandong	RMB 148,349.25 yuan
Zheng's Wealth	Beijing	RMB 132,484.72 yuan
Baoyide	Shandong	RMB 55,539 yuan
WeiCi Finance	Guangdong	RMB 40,183.9 yuan
Juchuang Crowdfunding	Shandong	RMB 25,425.79 yuan
Zhongyi	Shandong	RMB 25,009.8 yuan
Dingsheng	Jiangsu	RMB 23,680.3 yuan
Jinniuzuo	Shandong	RMB 15,860.9 yuan
Xunxiao	Shandong	RMB 14,194.42 yuan
Taizhong Automobile Crowdfunding	Zhejiang	RMB 14,030.61 yuan
Rongpinhui	Shandong	RMB 13,670 yuan
Tongqian	Shandong	RMB 11,968 yuan
Chuangke Tianxia	Shandong	RMB 10,876.1 yuan
Zhirenke	Jiangsu	RMB 10,770.97 yuan
Benkeda	Hebei	RMB 10,182 yuan
887 Crowdfunding	Shandong	RMB 8416.99 yuan
Carrmb	Jiangsu	RMB 6697.94 yuan
Jiachehui	Shandong	RMB 6651.95 yuan
Xingzhe	Shanghai	RMB 4775.84 yuan
Mili Crowdfunding	Anhui	RMB 4552.5 yuan

Data Source www.yingcanzixun.com

are located in Shandong, which reveals the fast development of automobile crowdfunding there (Table 4.3).

4.2.7 Financing Status of Automobile Crowdfunding Platforms

According to a quarterly statistics of Yingcanzixun, by the end of September 2016, two automobile crowdfunding platforms have obtained venture capital investment, including WeiCi Finance and Xingfami, and WeiCi Finance has completed two rounds of financing.

- **WeiCi Finance's Two Rounds of Financing**

As reported,[8] WeiCi Finance obtained several million angel investment from Xinjin Capital in July 2015. On May 3, 2016, WeiCi Finance further announced that it

[8]WeiCi Finance: http://www.weiclicai.com/article/86.

completed its Pre-A round financing over RMB 10 million, with Gobi Partners as the lead investor, and Rushan Investments and Fenghou Capital as the following investors. WeiCi Finance is a crowdfunding platform focusing on automobile industry, with the primary projects on the used car at present. WeiCi Finance went online on September 2015, and by the end of September 2016, the platform had cumulatively raised RMB 401 million.

- **Xingfami Received Strategic Investment of RMB 3 Million**

In April 2016, Xingfami announced its receipt of a strategic investment of RMB 3 million from some well-known investors.[9] Xingfami, a subsidiary of Fami (Shenzhen) Internet Finance Co. Ltd., is a crowdfunding platform focusing on used car industry, which went online on April 18, 2015. In its early development stage, the firm focused on mortgage loans, and, later, shifted to used car crowdfunding. By the end of September 2016, Xingfami had 188 crowdfunding projects, with accumulatively raised fund amount up to RMB 45.24 million.

4.2.8 The Existing Risks of Used Car Crowdfunding

Automobile crowdfunding is featured with relatively shorter investment period and higher rate of return. However, risks always go with investment and returns, and the higher the return, the higher the risk. In general, automobile crowdfunding may possess the following risks:

(1) Moral Risk

The moral risk is primarily triggered by platforms and vehicle dealers or the project initiators. There exist fraud crowdfunding platforms as incurred in the P2P online lending platforms. Automobile crowdfunding is a newly developed field without government regulations in place yet, but with the low threshold and low fraud cost. As a result, some platforms may come to this industry purely for fraud without any real and substantial business projects. They could deliberately mislead the potential investors with fake promises of high returns. Therefore, investors need to be cautious when choosing platforms and projects.

(2) Incomplete Disclosure of Information by Platform

As all the investors of used cars crowdfunding are "netizens", and most of them can only obtain very limited information about the cars through platform, such as vehicle pictures and whatever information published on platform's websites, and will not be able to really know the actual conditions of vehicles, such as the previous accidents. In addition, the regulations have not imposed any requirements on information disclosure for crowdfunding platforms at present, so the investors

[9]NetEase News: http://money.163.com/16/0419/17/BL1IA64E00253B0H.html.

have to make their decisions based on incomplete disclosure of information for the used cars.

(3) Selection and Sales Risks of Used Cars

The selection and sales risks primarily come from pre-investment review risk of the platforms, and the post-investment sales risk of the used cars. For the pre-investment review risk, the platforms may not adopt some high-enough standards to allow the used vehicles to be listed on the platforms. For the sales risk, the investors may not be able to identify and trace the used cars with defects in the market. In particular, the following three types of defective vehicles may generate sales risk for the investors:

A. Pledged Vehicles

If the vehicles for trading have been pledged for loans or other transactions, then, these vehicles, by law, cannot be sold and transferred. This may result in investors' funds to be frozen.

B. Vehicles Repaired with Previous Accidents

Investors may not be able to know the vehicle's maintenance history and specific accident information through platforms. Compared with "normal" vehicles, the vehicles that was repaired after accidents typically have higher possibility of having accidents again, which may seriously influence the value of the used cars, and cause the loss of investors.

C. Vehicles with Illegal Ownership

The vehicles with illegal ownership refer to these stolen and smuggled vehicles or those without complete registration documentations. Due to the high price-performance ratio, these vehicles with illegal ownership may attract some used-car dealers and crowdfunding platforms. However, once the legitimacy issue of these vehicles are disclosed, the used cars could be taken away by law enforcement authority, and investors' investment funds could be lost.

(4) Inadequate Regulatory Policies

As a newly developed industry, the regulations on the used car crowdfunding industry is not in place yet. As a result, investors may be less effectively protected when the disputes incurred, while the setup of any new regulation may also cause the loss of investors if the current practice is not consistent with the new rules and regulations.

4.2.9 Summary

In 2016, automobile crowdfunding, led by Shandong Province, exhibited a rapid growth. As a newly developed way of financing, crowdfunding for used cars and the imported vehicles through non-national-general dealers could truly help solve the short term liquidity issue of the car dealers, and meanwhile, provide investors with the opportunity of obtaining considerable investment returns. So far, the used car crowdfunding has attracted more than 360,000 investors, and nearly 15,000 used cars are successfully traded through crowdfunding platforms. Considering there are about 5 million used cars being traded through traditional channels in the first half year of 2016, the potential for the used car crowdfunding market is tremendous. With the implementation of regulatory rules on P2P online lending industry and exit of more and more smaller online lending platforms, the automobile crowdfunding, as an temporarily un-regulated industry, may become an outlet for these transferred P2P lending platforms.

At the same time, as an un-regulated industry, automobile crowdfunding possesses many risks due to the lack of regulations, and the qualifications of different platform are totally uneven. The news about platform's run-away can be heard from time to time. As an extreme example, Jinfu Online, a used car crowdfunding platform, ran away only 9 days after its operation in August 2016.[10] Therefore, the investors in used car crowdfunding industry need to be very cautious when they make their investment decisions.

4.3 Physical Store Crowdfunding

With the rapid growth of crowdfunding, more and more companies with physical stores are choosing this innovative way of financing to raise funds. Among them, the physical stores focusing on catering and entertainment with some unique operating and profiting models notably stand out, and are also favored by a large number of investors.

4.3.1 The Background and Rationales

As the income level of average consumers grow with the development of Chinese economy, more and more people start to pay attention to the quality of their lives, and consumers' demands for various consumption goods and services are becoming increasingly stronger ever, especially for the demands on catering, recreational activities and travel accommodations. According to the National Bureau of Statistics,[11] the revenue from catering industry in China broke the record of RMB 3 trillion for the first time in 2015, which was about RMB 3.2310 trillion, increasing by 11.7% on a year-over-year basis. In addition, on March 23, 2016,

---

[10]http://auto.sohu.com/20160922/n468993267.shtml.

[11]National Bureau of Statistics: http://www.stats.gov.cn/tjsj/zxfb/201602/t20160229_1323991.html, http://www.stats.gov.cn/tjsj/zxfb/201602/t20160229_1323991.html.

China's Ministry of Finance and the State Administration of Taxation issued the Notice on Implementation of the Pilot Program of Substitution of Income Tax with Value-added Tax.[12] The Notice states that, from May 1, 2016, a pilot program will be implemented to substitute income tax with the value-added tax, covering the industries of construction, real estate, finance, and services. As a part of the service industry, catering and accommodation sub-industries are certainly included within the scope of the pilot program. As a result, the overall tax of catering and accommodation industries are expected to be reduced, which is undoubtedly a good news for these industries.

However, investment in these industries by opening the physical stores may require large amount of funding, from hundreds of thousands of yuan to millions of yuan, but the project initiators are typically individuals, who, usually, only have limited funding source, and difficulties in obtaining finance through traditional financing channels. The rise and development of crowdfunding, in this case, will provide these small business owners with a new and convenient channel of financing, and at the same time, supply them with an effective way of marketing and sales as well. Physical stores plus Internet crowdfunding is just a product of market needs under this industrial environment.

4.3.2 The Return Model and Exit Mechanism

(1) The Return Model

Physical store crowdfunding refers to a model that investors will obtain certain equity or other returns through their invested funds in stores, and help the project initiators open stores or expand business. The investment fields may cover leisure, entertainment and other service industries, such as catering, accommodations, gymnasium clubs, KTV, and education. At present, the catering and accommodation take the majority of the investment fields, and their operational model and procedures are basically the same as those of non-public equity financing projects.

There are multiple ways of providing returns to investors for physical store crowdfunding, which may include physical return, equity dividend, and other types of yields. Physical return usually takes the form of consumer discount cards or products of crowdfunded stores, such as coupons, discount cards, entrance tickets and experiential activity tickets of crowdfunded stores, which are often combined with other ways of returns; equity dividend refers to obtaining some shares of physical stores as a return for investors after crowdfunding succeeds, and receiving a portion of profits according to the portion of equity shares that the investors hold; and the yields can be divided into fixed yield and floating yield, and the floating yield refers to the sum of basic fixed yield plus profit sharing or dividend payout. In

[12]http://szs.mof.gov.cn/zhengwuxinxi/zhengcefabu/201603/t20160324_1922515.html.

Table 4.4 Forms of returns

Return models	Form
Physical returns	Consumer discount cards or products of crowdfunding stores, such as coupons, discount cards, entrance tickets and experiential activity tickets of crowdfunding stores
Equity dividend return	Obtain some equity shares of physical stores as return after crowdfunding succeeds, and share profits according to the proportion of shares owned
Yield return	1. Fixed yield 2. Floating yield: basic yield (such as 12%, annualized) * non-repurchased investment amount + floating yield (say, 4% * operation income) * non-repurchased investment amount

Data Source www.yingcanzixun.com

terms of the ways of returns, equity return and yield return are the primary forms of returns at present (Table 4.4).

It is worth noting that, when some physical store crowdfunding projects distribute dividends as the way of returns, the project initiators or the management teams of physical stores will also receive a certain proportion of dividends for their management shares, typically, 10–20% of the total dividends payout. For physical store crowdfunding projects, the dividends are usually distributed quarterly or semi-annually, but some projects may distribute dividends or share profit monthly.

(2) The Exit Mechanism

The physical store crowdfunding projects, such as catering projects, are quite different from other equity crowdfunding projects, as the investors of the physical store crowdfunding do not pursue the public listing or next round of financing as the ways of exit; instead, they are looking for the profit sharing as the way of returns, which is similar to other types of consumption crowdfunding projects where the liquidation, ownership transfer or buy-back after the lockout period are the common practice (Table 4.5).

4.3.3 Some Statistics of Physical Store Crowdfunding

(1) The Number of Physical Store Crowdfunding Platforms by Province in China

According to a quarterly statistics of Yingcanzixun, by the end of September 2016, there were 61 physical store crowdfunding platforms under normal operating conditions in China, including 40 comprehensive physical store crowdfunding platforms, and 21 vertical physical store crowdfunding platforms. These physical store crowdfunding platforms are located in 14 provinces and cities, among them, Beijing, Guangdong and Zhejiang rank the top three, with 18, 17, and 7 platforms, respectively; Shanghai ranks the fourth, with 6 platforms. The number of physical store crowdfunding platforms in the top four areas accounts for 78.69% of the total number of physical store crowdfunding platforms in China. It happened, simply

Table 4.5 Some examples of ways of return and exit

Project	Return model	Exit mechanism
Yuhua Western Restaurant Xixiang Store	1. Basic yield of investors: 10% * investment amount, by month 2. Extra yield of investors: 0.5% * operating revenue * proportion of remaining investment amount, by quarter 3. Any investor can have a coupon with face value of RMB 1000	1. Two-year blackout period 2. One-time repurchase after the blackout period
Xiangwang Xiangqing (Shenzhen Shajing Store)	1. 40% of shares are transferred, and profit is distributed by month. If the accumulative distributable profit within 1.5 years reaches RMB 1.8 million or above, then from the year 1.5 years after the establishment of the store, profit will be distributed to leading investor and other investors first, and project initiators will not participate in profit distribution. After the leading investor and other investors recover cost, the distributable profit of the project will be distributed according to the actual contribution proportion of each party 2. Investors can obtain 1% of consumption coupon with value of 1% of investment amount each month	1. The shares are not allowed to be transferred within one year. But it can be transferred after one year, and can be transferred once for every six months later 2. Liquidation 3. If the store can't be operated continuously or the lease contract can't be renewed after expiration due to the reasons of the project initiators, then the project initiators will repurchase all shares
Meet Fresh (Including all stores of Beijing Baiweiyi Group)	1. 10% of shares are transferred, 1% will be returned each month, and dividend will be distributed once a year 2. Individual investors with investment amount above RMB 50,000 can obtain 20 free exchange certificates with face value of RMB 20 and 20 cash coupons with face value of RMB 5	Investors can exit one year later, and the store will be repurchased back according to investment principal after expiration

(continued)

Table 4.5 (continued)

Project	Return model	Exit mechanism
Xishuashua Chafing Dish Tianhong Mall Store	1. The project initiator holds 30% of shares (including 10% of management shares) and investors hold 70% of shares. Both parties can have the net profit dividend of the crowdfunding store according to the investment proportion 2. Shareholders can enjoy a discount of 20%	Repurchase is not promised
Huangtai Northwest Noodles (Shenzhen Futian Store)	1. Distributable profit of the project will be distributed once a month according to investment proportion 2. The regular investors need to transfer 20% of dividend to the project initiators and leading investor	The project is not allowed to be transferred within one year. It can be transferred after one year, and can be transferred once every six months later

Data Source www.yingcanzixun.com

because the economies are relatively developed in these areas, and the crowdfunding is also active there. Consequently, there are tremendous demands on catering and accommodation in these areas, and many of the smaller-sized suppliers that were set up to satisfy these demands were financed through crowdfunding (Fig. 4.25).

(2) Fundraising Scale of Physical Store Crowdfunding Platforms by Provinces in China

According to a quarterly statistics of Yingcanzixun, by the end of September 2016, the physical store crowdfunding platforms in China have successfully raised RMB 1.93 billion. Among them, Beijing ranks the first, with RMB 1.358 billion;

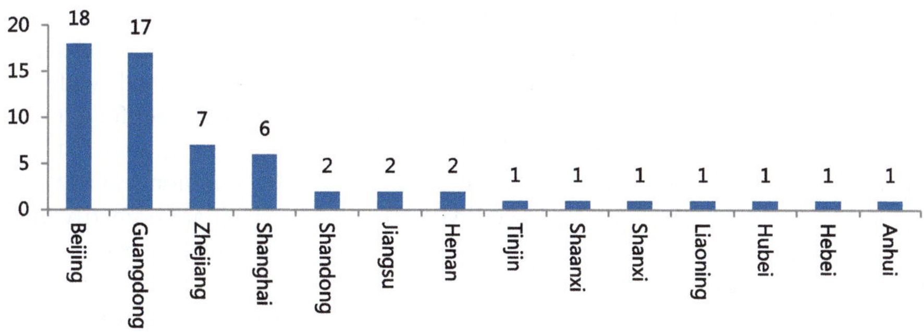

Fig. 4.25 Number of physical store crowdfunding platforms by provinces in China. *Data Source* www.yingcanzixun.com

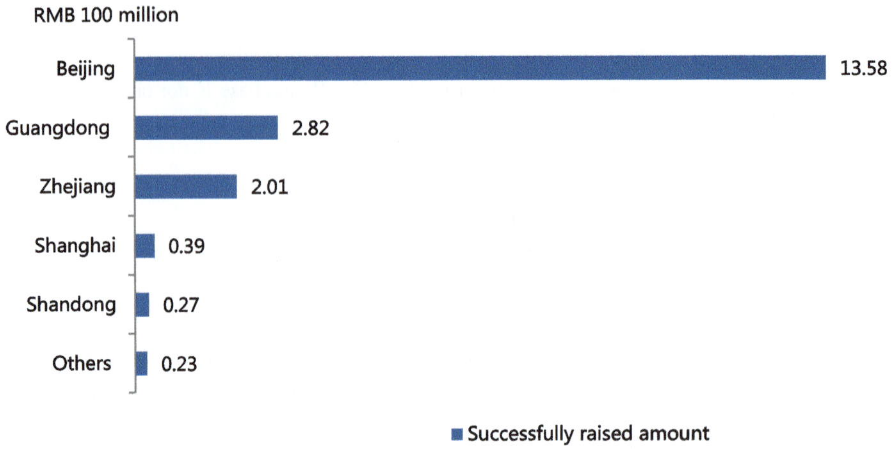

Fig. 4.26 Fundraising status of physical store crowdfunding by provinces in China. *Data Source* www.yingcanzixun.com

followed by Guangdong, with raised funds up to RMB 282 million; Zhejiang ranks the third with RMB 201 million; and Shanghai and Shandong rank the fourth and the fifth, with the raised amount up to RMB 39 million and RMB 27 million, respectively. The total raised funds by the physical store crowdfunding of the above five areas account for 98.8% of the total amount of funds raised by physical store crowdfunding in China. In particular, the amount raised by the physical store crowdfunding in Beijing alone accounts for 70.35% of the total amount of funds raised. In contrast, the other non-top-five provinces and cities only raised RMB 23 million in total, accounting for 1.2% of the total amount raised (Fig. 4.26).

(3) The Successful Physical Store Crowdfunding Projects by Funds Raised Amount

According to a quarterly statistics of Yingcanzixun, by the end of September 2016, there were 991 successful physical store crowdfunding projects in China. The number of projects with the fund raised amount between RMB 1 million and RMB 5 million appears as the largest, with 513 projects, accounting for 51.77% of the total number of successful projects; the number of projects with the fund raised amount between RMB 500,000 and RMB 1 million ranks the second, with 234 projects, accounting for 23.61%; the number of projects with the fund raised amount between RMB 100,000 and RMB 500,000 ranks the third, with 151 projects; there were 51 projects that raised funds between RMB 5 million and RMB 10 million, 25 projects raised funds above RMB 10 million, which are primarily hotel projects; and the number of projects with the fund raised amount below RMB 100,000 is the least, with only 17 projects. It seems that most successful physical store crowdfunding projects have the fund raised amount between RMB 500,000 and RMB 5 million, accounting for 75.38% of the total number of the projects. The projects with fund raised amount within this range are primarily the well-operated

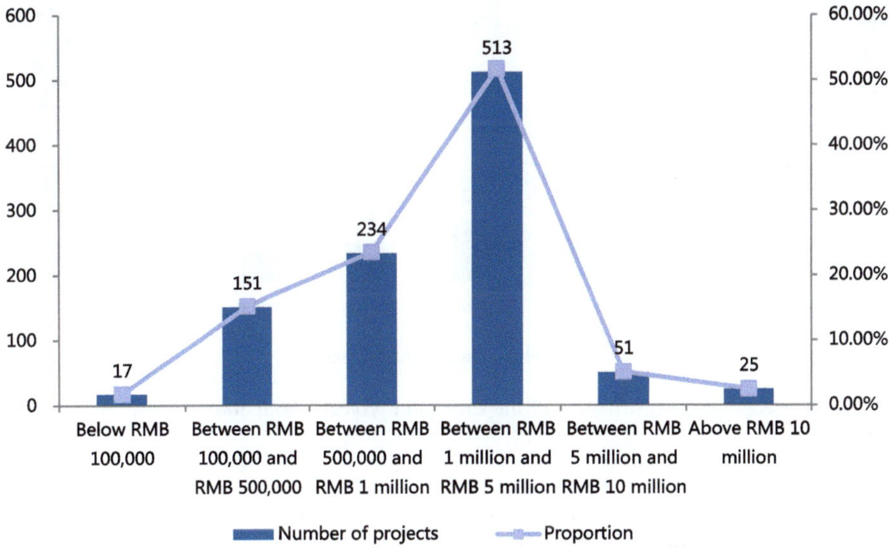

Fig. 4.27 The successful physical store crowdfunding projects by raised fund amount. *Data Source* www.yingcanzixun.com

existing independent stores or chain stores, and investors showed higher enthusiasm towards these physical store projects (Fig. 4.27).

(4) Geographical Distribution of the Successful Projects

For the geographical distribution of the successful physical store crowdfunding projects, Guangdong ranks the top with 190 successful projects; followed by Beijing, with 173 successful projects; Shanghai ranks the third with 89 successful projects; Shandong and Anhui rank the fourth and the fifth, with 82 successful projects and 51 successful projects, respectively; the numbers of successful projects are almost the same for Henan and Zhejiang, with 43 projects and 40 projects, respectively; and the rest of the 22 provinces and cities have 323 successful projects in total. The number of successful projects of the top five provinces and cities accounts for 59.03% of the total number of successful projects, which is primarily because these are the relatively developed areas with higher population density, high living standard, and stronger consumption demands (Fig. 4.28).

4.3.4 The Financing Status of Vertical Physical Store Crowdfunding Platforms

As of the end of September 2016, there were 3 vertical physical store crowdfunding platforms that had obtained venture capital investment, including Zhongchouke,

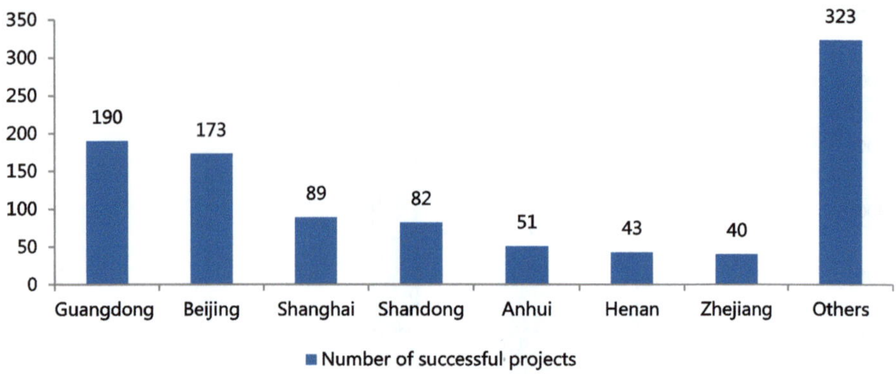

Fig. 4.28 Geographical distribution of the successful projects. *Data Source* www.yingcanzixun.com

Huimeng Zone and Duocaitou. Among them, Zhongchouke and Duocaitou already completed two rounds of financing.

- **Zhongchouke Completed Two Rounds of Financing**

Zhongchouke is a physical store online equity crowdfunding platform focusing on catering and entertainment industries, and a subsidiary of Beijing Zhongchouke Network Technology Co., Ltd.[13] In July 2015, Zhongchouke announced its receipt of angel investment of about RMB 10 million from multiple institutional and individual investors, including KRC Investment and the famous angel investor Song Yuhai. On March 23, 2016, Zhongchouke further announced its successful financing from an A-round investment of tens of millions of yuan, led by Neo Capital and followed by multiple individual investors.

- **Huimeng Zone's Pre-A-Round Investment of RMB 15 Million**

Huimeng Zone is a consumer service crowdfunding platform focusing on catering industry, which officially went online in June 2015.[14] On May 12, 2016, Huimeng Zone announced publicly that it received a Pre-A-round financing of RMB 15 million, and the investment was led by Qiantong Capital and followed by some professional investors.

- **Duocaitou Completed Two Round of Financing**

Duocaitou is a crowdfunding platform focusing on boutique hotel and accommodation industry, which adopts the spatial crowdfunding model of "PE + Crowdfunding".[15] In July 2015, Duocaitou announced that it obtained

[13]Zhongchouke. http://www.zhongchouke.com/help-index.htm.

[14]Gather Power to Realize Dreams: Huimeng Zone Obtains Pre-A-round Strategic Investment, May 12, 2016, http://www.hmzone.com/news/20160512105443.html.

[15]Duocaitou: http://www.duocaitou.com/main/news.

Table 4.6 Financing status of vertical physical store crowdfunding platforms

Platform	Financing time	Round	Investor	Financing amount
Zhongchouke	July 2015	Angel round	Multiple institutions and individuals, including KRC investment and the famous angel investor Song Yuhai	Nearly RMB 10 million
Duocaitou	July 2015	Angel round	Shuiwei Capital, a subsidiary of Lei Jun's Xiaomi Group	Ten-million level
Zhongchouke	March 2016	A round	Neo Capital leads the investment and multiple individual investors follow the lead investment	Ten-million level
Huimeng Zone	May 2016	Pre-A round	Qiantong Capital leads the investment and professional investors follow the lead investment	RMB 15 million
Duocaitou	August 2016	Pre-A round	Innovation Angel Funds, Shared Capital and Shuiwei Capital	Ten-million level

Data Source www.yingcanzixun.com

ten-million-level angel investment from Shuiwei Capital. On August 8, 2016, it further announced that it had completed ten-million-level Pre-A-round financing with fund from Innovation Angel Funds, Shared Capital and Shuiwei Capital (Table 4.6).

4.3.5 The Existing Risks

As the crowdfunded stores are becoming more and more popular, the issues of poor profitability and low degree of transparency of these crowdfunded stores also appear to the general public, and some crowdfunded stores, such as Impressive Xiangjiang Century City Store in Changsha, even went bankruptcy by closing down the store for liquidation.[16] As a new way of financing, there is no question that the physical store crowdfunding exhibits several risks.

(1) The Moral Risk

The moral risk is primarily embodied in project initiators. As the regulations for the industry are still not in place yet at present, the entry barrier for this market is relatively low and defrauding cost is low as well. The project initiators may defraud by providing false accounting/financial information, use the obtained funds for other purposes, or even run away with obtained funds.

[16]http://hunan.sina.com.cn/news/2015-11-01/detail-ifxkhcfn4247079.shtml.

(2) The Imperfect Operation of Platforms

The operations of physical store crowdfunding platforms, from the pre-review process to post-investment management, is still far from perfect at present. As the investors, usually, cannot directly assess the validity of projects, it is extremely critical for the platforms to conduct adequate due diligence for the submitted projects in early stage. However, the standards that are adopted by platforms for due diligence and entry permit may not be adequate at present, as a result, there is a possibility that some listed projects may not possess the quality as they claimed, and some project initiators may provide false information, but not being identified by the platforms' due diligence review process. In addition, the post-investment management and monitoring mechanism of the platforms may not be adequate either, so the project initiators may conduct some illegal activities, such as concealing their true financial status, providing false information, and embezzling funds, without being found by the platforms and investors in a timely manner. The investors, in reality, usually do not actively monitor the actual status of the invested projects after investment, instead, only concern about profit sharing and distributions.

(3) The Market Risk

The success of the crowdfunded physical stores is closely related to their site locations and market positioning. Whether the market positioning and customer segmentations of the physical stores fit with their respective market niche is the key for their success. Improper positioning and segmentation may lead to the failure of the crowdfunded physical stores.

(4) The Management Risk

Some project initiators do not have the relevant business experience and management skills previously in the industry, and do not possess adequate product innovation ability, either. In particular, there are typically lack of standardized and effective management systems, financial controls and operating procedures in these traditional physical stores. As a result, it may lead to a sequence of financial issues, such as nontransparent financial accounts, undisclosed use of funds, and uncontrolled operating cost of the stores.

(5) The Policy Risk

On October 13, 2016, the State Council formally issued the Notice on the Implementation of Special Rectification on Internet Financial Risks. The Notice clearly stated that the equity crowdfunding platforms are prohibited to publish any fake or false bids, raise funds for the platforms themselves, issue debt in the name of equity funding, or raise funds in any disguised form; and the platforms should fully disclose information and protect investors' interests by not releasing any false statements and running any misleading promotion activities. In reality, however, some physical store crowdfunding projects indeed raise funds by debt instrument but in the name of equity investment, which didn't comply with the policy requirements and incurred the policy risks.

(6) The Lack of Regulations

At present, the regulations on the crowdfunding have not been in place yet. In particular, the laws and regulations on equity crowdfunding have not been set up. Under this condition of lack of regulations, the investors' interests may not be adequately protected when any possible incidents incurred.

4.3.6 Summary

In summary, as the people's living standard improves over time, consumers' demands for both products and services and the needs to finance their consumptions are growing as well. The emergence of the crowdfunding provides consumer service industry with a new financing path to address the long-existing issue of difficulties in financing lower-income consumers and smaller-sized providers of consumer goods and services. However, the growth of the physical store crowdfunding is still relatively slow to get to this point. By the end of September 2016, about RMB 1.876 billion has been raised, which may indicate that the great potential and faster development of the industry are still down the road. At present, the physical store crowdfunding still encounters the various types of risks, insufficient operating capability, and lack of regulations. Many listed projects may not possess the needed quality and value for the potential investors, and many projects failed even with the successful fundraising. Therefore, the investors of the physical store crowdfunding need to be cautious when choosing projects, and had better not to be a "hands-off" investor; instead, should keep close eyes on monitoring the invested projects.

4.4 Agricultural Crowdfunding

As the concept of "Internet +" becomes more and more popular, more industries are involved in this "internet plus" process. Among many industries that actively embraced the crowdfunding, agricultural is just a new example of this growing trend.

Agriculture crowdfunding was not initiated in China, instead, stemmed from the US. The well-known overseas agricultural crowdfunding platforms include Fquare and Agfunder. Fquare is a crowdfunding platform that was set up in 2012 focusing on farmland.[17] Through Fquare, the investors can purchase the "shares" of the lands that they selected, and the previous farmer/owner will became the tenants of the farmland after they sell the farmland to the investors. The farmlands were held and managed by

[17]http://crowdlanding.com/platform_profile.php?id=85.

a third party entity, Peoples Realty Company LLC, which leases lands to the farmers and collects rents from the farmers. On the other hand, the investors can sell their shares in the secondary market when they determine to exit from their investment.

Agfunder is an agricultural crowdfunding platform focusing on agricultural products and technologies.[18] Agfunder selected less than 2% of companies that apply for listing to post on its crowdfunding platform, and the investors can invest for their selected projects as little as $10,000. For the investors who wish to diversify their investment, Agfunder provides the opportunity of portfolio investment by setting up a managed fund led by AgFunder investment professionals. The portfolio investors can gain access to exclusive, unlisted investment opportunities with minimum investment amount of $100,000. In addition, Agfunder also welcome institutional investors to participate and lead the investment. So far, Agfunder has helped 16 companies raise over $34 million from over 3000 accredited investors.

In China, the first vertical agricultural crowdfunding platform, Taste Fresh,[19] went online in March 2014, and Taste Fresh is an agricultural crowdfunding platform that provides an one-stop-shopping service for the customers, including finance, investment, incubation and operations. According to a quarterly statistics of Yingcanzixun, by the end of September 2016, there were 10 crowdfunding platforms focusing solely on agricultural crowdfunding, and 53 comprehensive crowdfunding platforms with agricultural projects with total raised fund amount up to RMB 534 million.

4.4.1 The Rise of Agricultural Crowdfunding

From "clenbuterol", "gutter oil" (illicit cooking oil) to toxic rice, poison bean sprouts and "long-frozen meat" (with chemicals to maintain the normal appearance), food safety incidents frequently appeared as the top line stories of various medias in China in the recent years. As a result, more and more consumers started to pay more attention to food safety issue, and begin to seek solutions for getting safer and healthier foods. In reality, however, consumers in China today seem powerless in identifying the safer food.

On the other hand, as some news reported in the recent years, many quality, safe and healthy agricultural products cannot be sold in the market in a timely manner. Millions of kilograms of brand pears were stuck in the warehouses; a large number of unsold nectarines were poured into the river of the villages; and acres of watermelons just rot in land fields. Farmers often have high yield of crops but not decent monetary income. While people living in urban areas complain about the high price of vegetables and fruit, huge quantity of agricultural products cannot be sold out in the market, even with a low price. The information asymmetry makes it

[18]https://agfunder.com/#/.

[19]http://www.zhongchou.com/deal-show/id-2704, www.changxianzhongchou.com.

difficult for farmers to sell their agricultural products, and, at the same time, makes it hard for consumers in urban areas to purchase these agricultural products. And the agricultural crowdfunding arises as a possible solution to tackle this challenge.

4.4.2 *The Agricultural Crowdfunding Models*

Agricultural crowdfunding falls into the category of reward crowdfunding with agricultural products as rewards. Agricultural crowdfunding can be found in the agricultural modules of many crowdfunding platforms, such as Taobao Crowdfunding, JD Crowdfunding, and Suning Crowdfunding. The agricultural crowdfunding typically takes two forms—"Group Purchase + Pre-Orders" and "Customized Production".

The "Group Purchase + Pre-Orders" Model

The most common form of agricultural crowdfunding is the "Group Purchase + Pre-Orders". As the scope of the agricultural products using crowdfunding is relatively limited, the major products posted on the platforms are typically some local specialty agricultural products or healthy green foods. The crowdfunding procedure is same as those of the general reward crowdfunding: Project initiators launch crowdfunding projects, and platforms review the submitted projects. The submitted projects will be posted on the platforms if they pass the review process. Then, the investors can choose their favorable products with desirable rewards to invest. If the crowdfunding succeeds, then projects will be carried out, and the investors will obtain the corresponding rewards or returns. On the other hand, if crowdfunding fails, the funds will be returned back to the account of investors.

"Customized Production" Model

"Customized Production" crowdfunding refers to raising funds for the project initiators to invest in farms or the ownership of some targeted agricultural products, and the investors can obtain the leasing right of farms and the ownership of some agricultural products within a pre-specified period of time, instead of the ownership of entire farms, with the agricultural products, or income, or right of farm visiting and farming experience as the rewards or returns. For example, if an investor invests in a piece of land or an ownership of a fruit tree or a sheep for a certain period of time, he/she does not need to plant on the farmland or breed the animals by him/herself, instead, the real farmers will do these jobs for them according to the agreement and the requirements of the investors, and deliver the requested products to investors after the harvest. The investors are also entitled to visit farms or experience the farming or breeding process. The actual crowdfunding procedure is as follows: the project initiators launch the crowdfunding, and platforms review the submitted projects. The projects will go online if they pass the review process, and then, the investors start to select and invest if they are interested. If crowdfunding succeeds, farmers will plant or breed according to the needs of the investors, and investors can also monitor the farming process in details in real time through the internet. Finally, the farmers will deliver the requested agricultural products to investors after the harvest, and the investors receive their expected returns.

There is a difference between "Customized Production" and "Group Purchase + Pre-Orders" crowdfunding, even though the Customized Production also takes the form of agricultural products as rewards or returns. For "Customized

Table 4.7 Agricultural crowdfunding projects

Project name	Part of returns	Return form
Winter is coming, Ginger is needed	Any investor who successfully invests RMB 18 in project can obtain 2.5 kg of fresh ginger with an original price of RMB 35	Agricultural products
Be the master of pre-rain-season tea of the unique Longjing Tea Garden	1. If investing RMB 69, the investor can obtain the ownership of pre-rain-season Longjing Tea yield from 40 20-year old Meijiawu Longjing tea trees (with tea land area 0.01 acre) for a quarter 2. If investing RMB 999 and raise funds for 400 50-year-old tea trees, the investor can obtain the ownership of pre-rain-season Longjing yield for three years. These trees can be repurchased back by 60% of market price, and the investor can obtain additional 75 kg pre-rain-season Longjing tea with a period of three years; and the investor can enjoy exclusive butler service with a value of RMB 298	Agricultural products + equity earnings
[Yushan Town] Qianshan "flying chicken" in bamboo forest, following the nature, in response to needs	1. If investing RMB 19, the investor can receive 10 fresh eggs laid by Yushan "flying chickens" 2. Any investor who invests in RMB 79 can subscribe a baby Yushan flying chick (the chick wears a foot ring with customer name) and raise it in Qianshan mountain of Qianxin Town. Investors need to pay management fee RMB 3.9 yuan each month for a raising period of 10–12 months, or the period can be determined by investors	Agricultural products

(continued)

Table 4.7 (continued)

Project name	Part of returns	Return form
[Exploration] Scenery in quiet countryside, forests better your health	1. Investors who invest RMB 19.9 yuan can obtain 10 well-selected super-grade lemons 2. Investors who invest RMB 1999 (at least three investors) can visit ecological farm four times a year for free and can contract a whole tree for picking up lemons	Agricultural products + visiting experience
Nameless Tea 3 Changbai Mountain has been leased by us, but only lack you—the king of forest	1. Investors who invest RMB 360 can lease a mulberry in a 100-year-old mulberry forest along the ancient Yellow River course for a year; obtain a can of mulberry leaf tea, a can of mulberry juice and a bag of dried mulberry; the investor can visit the old mulberry forest to pick up the remaining fruit on trees and experience the process of tea picking up and making tea at the end of spring and the beginning of summer 2. Any investor who invests RMB 50,000 can become the "king" who will have the naming right and control right to a mountain owned by Nameless Tea Group; the right of living in the wooden house in the nameless forest of Changbai Mountain for a year; obtain two cans of fresh tea of current season provided by Nameless Tea Group each quarter for five successive years; become the joint founder of Nameless Tea, and can participate in the Nameless Tea founders' annual meeting	Agricultural products + visiting experience + services

Data Source www.yingcanzixun.com

Production", crowdfunding comes first, followed by actual farming activities, with many forms of returns as mentioned above. For the "Group Purchase + Pre-Orders" crowdfunding, however, farming activities come first, followed by crowdfunding, and the primary form of returns is agricultural products.

Several examples of the agricultural crowdfunding projects with different return models are listed in Table 4.7.

4.4.3 *Some Advantages of Agricultural Crowdfunding*

(1) Food safety has been among the most concerned issues for consumers in China, as it is directly and closely related to consumers' health and wellbeing. The agricultural crowdfunding actually provides a way to help resolve the food safety issue to some extent. Through the agricultural crowdfunding process, the consumers can directly deal with agricultural producers without intermediate layers, and personally monitor the production process, which can significantly alleviate the risk that some agricultural products may be maliciously processed in a toxic way by some greedy merchants. At the same time, due to less intermediate layers, consumers will be able to consume not only safer, but also fresher agricultural products.
(2) The agricultural crowdfunding can also help increase the demands for agricultural products. In the recent years, the sluggish sales of agricultural products have caused farmers' severe losses, which badly impact farmers' confidence and willingness of continuing working in the agriculture industry. The agricultural crowdfunding, however, can effectively help expand the sales channels for the agricultural products. In particular, the "Customized Production" crowdfunding model will allow the farmers to make the production decisions after knowing the demands for their products, which can significantly reduce the degree of the information asymmetry, in addition to helping resolve the financing issues.
(3) The agricultural crowdfunding can also help enhance the consumer experience with the farmland life. For many consumers living in urban areas, they never got a chance to know how the agricultural products being produced and experience the farmland life. Through agricultural crowdfunding, however, these all become a reality. The consumers can not only obtain safer and healthier foods, but also can enjoy their "own" farm life experience. Many investors/consumers take their kids there to have a fun day in the farm for weekends and holidays.

4.4.4 *Summary*

From 2004 to 2016, the Chinese central government has issued the famous annual "Central Government Documentation No. 1" focusing on the issues of agriculture and rural areas for 13 consecutive years. The same issues were also discussed at the Fourth Session of China's Eleventh National People's Congress in 2016, and in the Outline of the 13th Five-Year Plan for the Economic and Social Development of

China that was approved by China's National People's Congress on March 17, 2016.[20] Among these prioritized items, the highlighted issues include the build-up of the agricultural supply chain and value chain, the establishment of a mechanism that can provide mutual benefits for all involved parties, the cultivation of the core companies with innovative integration models, the expansion of farmers' possible channels and sources to increase their incomes and share more benefits from value-added products, the encouragement and support of industrial and financial capital to be invested in modern agriculture, the development of new operating models such as the alliance between agriculture and business, and innovation in rural financial services.

However, the agricultural crowdfunding is not as popular as expected at present, even though the huge potential of agricultural industry is the consensus of the entire market. The relatively slow growth of the agricultural crowdfunding may be related to several possible factors, such as the scope of products that are restricted to some local specialty agricultural products, limited scope of the targeting investors/consumers, difficulties in transportation of some fresh agricultural products, bigger impact of natural disasters on agricultural products, as well as the long production cycles. As a result, developing some new ideas to resolve these existing issues are required for the future development of agricultural crowdfunding.

4.5 Real Estate Crowdfunding

According to a quarterly statistics of Yingcanzixun, by the end of September 2016, there were 19 crowdfunding platforms engaged in the real estate crowdfunding projects. Among them, 12 platforms are purely focusing on real estate crowdfunding, with the accumulatively raised funds up to RMB 1.2 billion. In contrast, as of the mid-April 2016, there were 30 crowdfunding platforms involved in the real estate crowdfunding projects, and 18 of which are purely focusing on the real estate crowdfunding platforms. Evidently, the scale of China's real estate crowdfunding platforms has declined greatly during a time span of about 5 months.

The changes in the real estate crowdfunding came up with the dynamics of the entire China's real estate market. In the past two years, China's real estate market has been widely considered with huge bubbles, and various types of speculative activities, including "speculation by crowdfunding" were observed in many places. As a result, the housing price of the major cities in China was driven to the roof, and triggered government controls by both central and local government.

On March 25, 2016, the General Office of Shenzhen Municipal Government issued the Opinions on Improving Subsidized Housing System and Promoting the

[20]http://www.gov.cn/xinwen/2016-03/17/content_5054992.html.

Stable and Healthy Development of Real Estate Market,[21] specifying that the government agencies will continue to carry out the investigation on financial risk and special rectification citywide based on an earlier assessment on the risks in the mortgage down payment. The financial institutions, such as internet financing firms and small-loan companies, are not allowed to be engaged in financial leveraging business, such as down payment loans, house purchasing through crowdfunding, and bridge loans. The industrial associations need to fully exert their self-regulating functions and guide internet financing firms and small-loan companies to operate in compliance with rules and policies, and the commercial banks are required to tighten the examinations on the source of down payment for house purchasing.

In response to the Notice of the Shenzhen Municipal Government, Shenzhen Internet Finance Association released The Notice of Shenzhen Internet Finance Association on Halting Real Estate Crowdfunding Business (hereinafter referred to as the “Notice”),[22] requiring all internet financing firms in the Shenzhen city to halt the real estate crowdfunding business, and conduct some self-examination and correctional activities. What’s more, the Notice specified that the scope of the real estate crowdfunding business include all crowdfunding businesses related to real estate, with the property forms including but not limited to non-governmental-subsidized commercial housing, stores, factory facilities, and apartments, and the crowdfunding models including but not limited to house purchasing through crowdfunding and house rental through crowdfunding. As a result, 8 real estate crowdfunding platforms registered in Shenzhen closed their businesses or stopped operations.

At present, there are three basic models adopted in real estate crowdfunding in China:

(1) The Wealth Management Model

The real estate crowdfunding is used as an option of investment to attract potential investors given the ever increasing housing price in China. If the value of the invested real estate property increases, then the investors can gain with considerable returns. Most housing properties listed on the platforms are non-performing asset obtained through auction, and the auction prices of these properties are usually only 70–80% of the market value of the houses. These real estate projects cover both residential and commercial properties, and this model is the mainstream one adopted by the real estate crowdfunding.

[21]General Office of Shenzhen Municipal People’s Government: Opinions on Improving Subsidized Housing System and Promoting the Stable and Healthy Development of Real Estate Market. SFB (2016) No. 12.

[22]Online Lending House: Shenzhen Internet Finance Association stops real estate crowdfunding and requires self-examination and self-correction, April 12, 2016, http://www.wdzj.com/news/zhengce/27938.html.

(2) Marketing and Sales Model

There are many ways of promoting sales of real estate properties through crowdfunding. For example, a house with 100 m^2 in size can be auctioned online from a base price, say RMB 500,000, and all the premium part, if any, will be distributed to the crowdfunding investors. The real estate companies often use the fixed yield, lottery drawing for houses, or auction of houses with discounted price as the target of the crowdfunding to promote sales of the houses, and the participants can obtain returns and discount through their investment in purchasing houses. In addition, the group purchase can allow the investors to use their investment to offset part of the house price when they purchase the houses, and provide convenience for the investors to visit the invested houses. These real estate projects are, in general, only involved in residential properties.

(3) Cooperative Building Model

Under this model, the targeting investors need to be first identified, and the land will be purchased after the investors and their needs are confirmed. This cooperative building model will provide the investors of the crowdfunding with the opportunities to participate in house design and development. As the crowdfunding will be launched when land is acquired, the costs of many intermediate layers, such as fees related with developer, financing, sales and inventory, can be significantly saved. These real estate projects, generally, also only involved in residential properties.

Chapter 5
Some Analysis on Several Leading Crowdfunding Platforms in China

Zhi Chen

In 2016, several developmental trends appeared in the reward crowdfunding and equity crowdfunding industries in China. On the one hand, the direction of the possible regulations became gradually clear, and the crowdfunding projects became more diverse and penetrated in more subdivided fields. On the other hand, the total number of platforms increased rapidly, the scale of the fundraising expanded sharply, and the investors showed increasingly higher enthusiasm to participate. In particular, with the support of the governmental policies, the ability of crowdfunding platforms in incubation of the innovative projects supported financially by crowdfunding is attracting increased attention from more and more market participants.

No matter it is currently a reward crowdfunding or equity crowdfunding, more and more platforms begin to realize that establishing collaboration with start-up ventures and forming resource-integrated ecology could be a more practical and sustainable long-term development model, compared with the current one of earning commissions only. Higher the ability of integrating resources of the platform, more likely being favored by state-up ventures to select as the listing platform. Reversely, if a crowdfunding platform loses its continuity in resource integration, and lacks the ability in innovation and incubation, it would be highly likely to be kicked out by the increasingly competitive crowdfunding market later or sooner.

Z. Chen (✉)
Shanghai Wenxi Investment Consulting Co., Shanghai, China
e-mail: chenzhi@wdzj.com

J.G. Wang et al. (eds.), *Financing from Masses*,
https://doi.org/10.1007/978-981-10-5843-1_5

5.1 JD Crowdfunding

5.1.1 Q1–Q3 2016: A Period of Rapid Growth for JD Crowdfunding

JD Crowdfunding is one of the five core businesses under JD Finance, and the fintech arm of JD.com that focuses on financial services.[1] The JD's crowdfunding business line was officially launched on July 1, 2014.

Since its inception, JD Crowdfunding has positioned itself as both a solution for start-ups and entrepreneurs to raise funding and an incubator that can help these companies grow. It aims to enable entrepreneurs and innovative start-ups to thrive, and help them deliver more diverse and exciting products for customers on JD.com.

JD Crowdfunding's offerings include rewards-based crowdfunding, equity crowdfunding and the JD Zhongchuang ecosystem, a one-stop-shopping platform providing entrepreneurs and innovative start-ups with the services and supports they need.

The rewards-based crowdfunding offering focuses on products in five key segments: smart transportation, household appliances, lifestyle, popular culture and charity. The goal of the platform is to encourage new ways of consumption and promote new cultural development trends. In October 2016, JD Crowdfunding launched an innovative new model matching IP (intellectual property) holders with producers and entrepreneurs. The "IP + Product" crowdfunding model leverages JD.com's huge e-commerce data base, and uses big data analysis of consumer demands to enable producers to identify high potential investment opportunities and connect the producers with IP rights holders.

Launched on March 31, 2015, JD Dongjia is a private equity financing service that leverages JD.com's diversified e-commerce businesses. It is dedicated to solving the difficulties that entrepreneurs and start-ups often face when they try to attract financing and investment. Currently, it covers two areas: investing in venture capital enterprises and consumption products. The venture capital enterprises adopt a "lead investment + follow-up investment" model to more effectively protect small-and-medium-sized investors, while the consumption products have a lower investment threshold and more stable earnings, targeting individual users.

The JD Zhongchuang Ecosystem offers a one-stop-shopping platform for all entrepreneurs and innovative start-ups to access JD resources, external investment, other services and training to support their growth.

Over the last two years, JD Crowdfunding and JD Zhongchuan have launched a diverse range of projects to help start-ups succeed. These projects include Raisers Alliance, Eyas Plan, Zhongchuang Service Platform, Zhongchuang College, "Hundred-Ten-One" Plan and Zhongchuang Ecology.

---

[1] https://z.jd.com/sceneIndex.html.

Table 5.1 JD reward-based crowdfunding—Q1–Q3 2016 results

JD rewards-based crowdfunding—Q1–Q3 2016 results	
Number of successful projects	2278
Total funds raised	RMB 1.376 billion

Data Source www.yingcanzixun.com

Table 5.2 JD Dongjia—Q1–Q3 2016 results

JD Dongjia—Q1–Q3 2016 results	
Total number of projects	43
Total funds raised	RMB 579 million

Data Source www.yingcanzixun.com

Under the "Hundred-Ten-One" Plan, JD Crowdfunding aims to invest in 100 start-ups, helping 10 of those reach a valuation of RMB 1 billion, and one of them achieve a valuation of RMB 10 billion (Table 5.1).

In the first three quarters of 2016, 43 successful projects on JD Dongjia raised more than RMB 500 million (Table 5.2).

5.1.2 How JD Crowdfunding Is Different

See Table 5.3.

Table 5.3 Features of JD crowdfunding

Features of JD crowdfunding and how it works	
Characteristic analysis	1. JD Crowdfunding is the first Chinese platform in the industry to offer fully integrated rewards-based crowdfunding, private equity financing and incubation services to help entrepreneurs access the funding they need to support innovation and growth Enterprises can use the rewards-based crowdfunding platform to raise initial seed financing, and then raise further funds through JD Dongjia as they grow in scale. At the same time, the JD Zhongchuang ecosystem provides access to JD.com's own resources covering investment, services and training, enabling startups to reduce time and costs when bringing their innovations to market. This strategy effectively improves the success rate of new projects, and makes it easier for entrepreneurs to develop their products
	2. JD Crowdfunding uses JD.com's innovative financial technology to support start-ups as they grow Leveraging JD Mall's huge data on e-commerce sales and partnerships with data analytical companies, JD Finance can analyze and identify trends in user preferences and consumer demand, providing invaluable insights that entrepreneurs can use to set up their business strategy and make their R&D efforts. These insights can also be used to create products and services in a more tailored way to satisfy the user needs

(continued)

Table 5.3 (continued)

Features of JD crowdfunding and how it works	
	3. JD Crowdfunding promotes a strategy called the "three new" concept. This refers to JD Crowdfunding's focus on creating new forms of consumption, promoting new cultural ideas, and encouraging new lifestyles
	4. "IP + product" crowdfunding model for cultural products The "IP + product" crowdfunding model leverages JD.com's huge e-commerce data base and use big data analysis of consumer demands to enable producers to identify high potential investment opportunities and connect the producers with IP rights holders At the same time, JD crowdfunding can also act as an incubator for these cultural projects, providing rewards-based crowdfunding, private equity financing and access to the Zhongchuang ecosystem

Data Source www.yingcanzixun.com

5.1.3 JD Crowdfunding's Profit Model

The rewards-based crowdfunding platforms usually charge a commission of 3% of funds raised. Similarly, the JD Dongjia platform collects a commission of 3% of total financing on amounts above RMB 10 million, and 5% on amounts less than RMB 10 million. JD Dongjia will also on occasion receive equity in the projects in lieu of commission, which enables financing companies to better apply the raised funds to growth initiatives.

5.2 Suning Crowdfunding

5.2.1 The Development of Suning Crowdfunding

The zc.suning.com, which was launched on April 16th, 2015, is a crowdfunding platform of Jinrong.suning.com focusing on consumption experience.[2] It offers a wide range of services from consumer payment, investment, consumer loans, crowdfunding, pre-paid card, insurance to corporate loans, among others. It's truly the very first platform focusing on consumption experience with both online platform and offline physical stores in China. The crowdfunding services include product crowdfunding and consumption crowdfunding, which cover the projects involving in technology, designing, charity, culture and entertainment, agriculture and real estate. The goal of the platform is to "support daily-life consumptions and dreams for fortune". The zc.suning.com devotes itself to create a multi-level ecosystem for the innovative and creative businesses.

[2]https://zc.suning.com/.

Table 5.4 Developmental of Suning crowdfunding

Developmental performance of Suning crowdfunding: April 2015–September 2016	
Total number of projects	937
Total amount of actually raised funds	RMB 1.074 billion

Data Source www.yingcanzixun.com

Since the launch of zc.suning.com until the end of September 2016, a totally RMB 1.074 billion has been raised with 3.396 million investors' participation in the crowdfunding activities, and 937 projects are already completed, among which there are 23 projects with over RMB 10 million raised and 64 projects with over RMB 1 million raised (Table 5.4).

5.2.2 *The Resources of zc.suning.com*

1. The multi-industrial background provides Suning with a massive consumer base. There are about 269 million users on suning.com, supported by about 1600 offline physical stores located in more than 600 cities inside and outside China.
2. The Suning Business Venture Camp supports young students of colleges and universities for their innovations through its incubation parks, which is headquartered in Nanjing, and setting up a pro-consumption territory and focusing on the incubation for the projects in cultural creativity, smart hardware and "Internet Plus".
3. Suning Youth Incubation Fund provides support for innovators, with up to RMB 300 million for young innovators at each stage of the growth cycle. The fund is primarily invested in the fields of technological development, consumption upgrade, intelligent manufacturing, culture and entertainment, computerized games, and other significant innovative concepts. So far, over 50 groups or firms have benefited from these investments.

5.2.3 *The Uniqueness of Sunning Crowdfunding*

For product crowdfunding, zc.suning.com adopts a special module of O2O. At the unique sections of "brands crowdfunding" and "competitive product resale", consumers can participate in the fund collecting not only online, but also at offline stores or Suning Wealth Centers located in Suning Plazas. In addition to the above "double line" funding, zc.suning.com also offers pioneering groups with the opportunities of participating in the Shanghai International Consumer Electronics Expo, CE China Exhibition and CES Exhibition. Through activities of online platform, offline stores, international exhibitions and other events, Suning helps incubation groups be exposed to general public and attract attentions from consumers, media and institutional investors.

In 2016, one of the Suning's crowdfunding projects Qishu Family Vertical Farm (a machine that helps vegetable growth) obtained support from 13,398 investors with raised fund of RMB 20.41 million through online crowdfunding, offline exhibition and experiential promotion at Suning stores, while its CiCi Little Chef's Fast Cooking Stove provides solutions of healthy and delicious cuisines for over 20,000 families, with a collected fund over RMB 15 million. Among product crowdfunding section of "brands crowdfunding" and "competitive product resale", the brands of DW watches, Zippo lighters and CityCoco intelligent skateboards are especially favored by the consumers.

In February 2016, "Xiaofeibao", a scenario-consumption crowdfunding, created the model of "earning money while consuming", which is pretty much a practice of "financing + production + consumption". During the process, consumers invest certain amount of funds in exchange for some consumption rights with value higher than the capitals they invested, and those investors who don't consume the products will receive monetary compensation in return, which created a brand new concept for investment and consumption. The "Xiaofeibao" in Jiangsu Province have received significant recognition from over 100,000 investors/consumers, with RMB 45 million raised funds.

5.2.4 The Profiting Model of Suning Crowdfunding

The Suning Crowdfunding charges a commission of 3% of raised funds for the launched projects from the projects initiators. For the unsuccessful crowdfunding projects within the pre-specified period, the platform will return the raised funds back to the accounts of investors. For the successful crowdfunding projects, the platform will first transfer part of the raised funds to the project initiators as the start-up funds. With the progress of projects, the platform will release more funds by installment according to the progress of the projects, so as to ensure that the investors' interests can be better protected. In the case that the rights and benefits of the investors cannot be delivered on time due to the issues caused by the project initiators, Suning crowdfunding platform will charge the project initiators additional 5% of raised funds as default penalty to compensate the investors.

5.3 Taobao Crowdfunding

5.3.1 The Development of Taobao Crowdfunding

As a subsidiary of Alibaba, Taobao Crowdfunding was launched by Taobao on March 1, 2014, with headquarters in Hangzhou, Zhejiang Province.[3] Taobao Crowdfunding involves in many industries, such as film and television, charity, book, entertainment, science and technology, design, cartoon, games, and agriculture. In the first three quarters of 2016, it successfully raised RMB 1.009 billion in total, with more than 3000 successful projects and, accumulatively, 16,204,700 investors (Table 5.5).

5.3.2 The Types of Taobao Crowdfunding

In the first three quarters of 2016, Taobao Crowdfunding successfully raised RMB 1.00857 billion in total, among which, science and technology crowdfunding collected the highest raised funds with RMB 685.72 million, accounting for 67.99% of the total raised amount; followed by agricultural crowdfunding, with raised amount of RMB 155.99 million, accounting for 15.47%; design crowdfunding ranked the third, with raised amount of RMB 96.47 million, accounting for 9.57%; cartoon crowdfunding ranked the fourth, and film and television crowdfunding ranked the fifth, with raised amount of RMB 20.57 million and RMB 7.33 million, respectively; charity crowdfunding and entertainment crowdfunding raised RMB 7.07 million and RMB 6.58 million, accounting for 0.7 and 0.65%, respectively; book crowdfunding raised RMB 1.03 million, accounting for 0.1%; and other types of crowdfunding raised RMB 27.81 million in total, accounting for 2.76% of the total raised amount (Fig. 5.1).

In the first three quarters of 2016, Taobao Crowdfunding totally engaged 16.2047 million investors. Among them, agricultural crowdfunding attracted the largest number of investors, up to 8.2825 million, accounting for 51.11% of the total number of investors; followed by science and technology crowdfunding, with 3.3372 million investors, accounting for 20.59%; design crowdfunding ranked the third with 1.14 million investors, accounting for 7.04%; followed by charity crowdfunding and cartoon crowdfunding with 369,400 and 142,000 investors, respectively; entertainment crowdfunding and film and television crowdfunding ranked the sixth and seventh with 86,600 and 47,100 investors, respectively; followed by book crowdfunding with 10,200 investors, only accounting for 0.06%; the other types of crowdfunding totally attracted 2.7896 million investors, accounting for 17.21% (Fig. 5.2).

[3]https://izhongchou.taobao.com/index.htm.

Table 5.5 Taobao crowdfunding: Q1–Q3 2016

Development of Taobao crowdfunding: Q1–Q3 2016	
Total number of projects	3294
Total amount of funds raised	RMB 1.009 billion
Number of investors	16,204,700

Data Source www.yingcanzixun.com

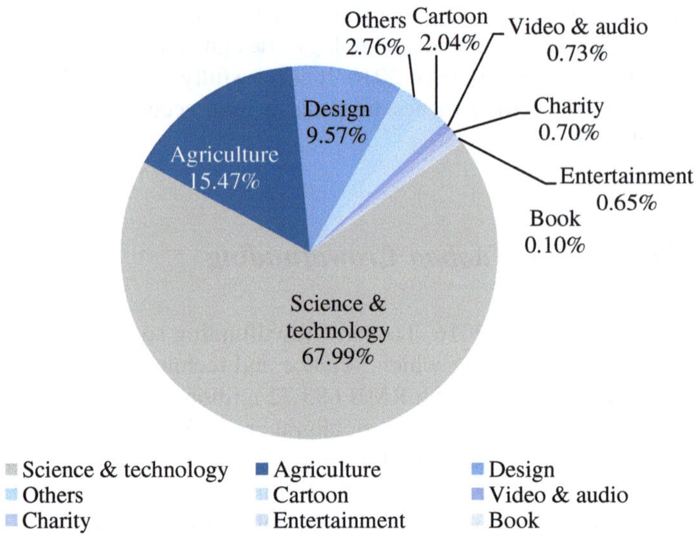

Fig. 5.1 Successfully raised amount of various types of Taobao crowdfunding. *Data Source* www.yingcanzixun.com

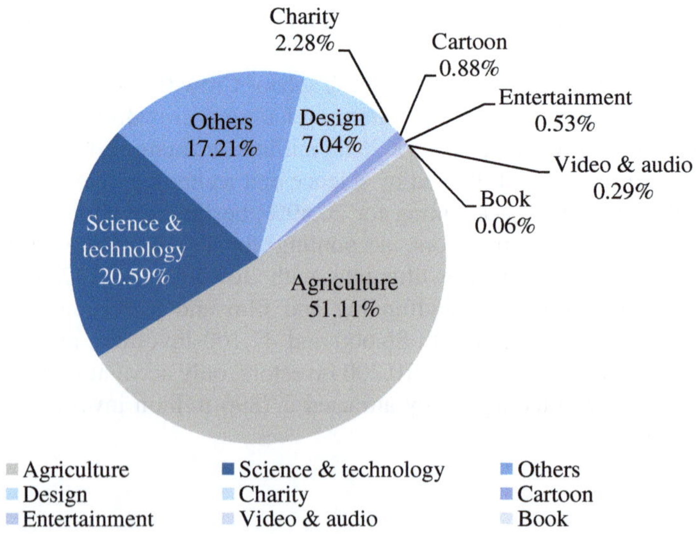

Fig. 5.2 Number of investors by various types of Taobao crowdfunding. *Data Source* www.yingcanzixun.com

5.3.3 The Features of Taobao Crowdfunding

See Table 5.6.

5.3.4 The Profiting Model of Taobao Crowdfunding

In contrast of many other crowdfunding platforms, Taobao Crowdfunding does not charge any service fees, and no profit sharing mechanism, either, with project initiators or investors.

5.4 Zhongtoubang

5.4.1 The Development of Zhongtoubang

Zhongtoubang is an online platform providing equity crowdfunding and other financing services with special focus on the firms listed on the National Equities Exchange and Quotations (NEEQ) and other firms that are planned to be listed.

Table 5.6 The features of Taobao crowdfunding

Characteristics of Taobao crowdfunding	
"Blind order"[a]	Taobao crowdfunding launches 700bike "blind order" on June 1, 2015. This is not only the first "blind order" project of Taobao, but also the first "blind order" crowdfunding project in China, which starts the age of blind order crowdfunding of China
New products	Taobao crowdfunding requires that all products sold through crowdfunding projects must be new products that haven't been sold yet through other channels or platforms
Imagination power	"Imagination power" is a brand marketing activity promoted by Taobao crowdfunding, which creates a super product each time
Entrepreneurs need a Taobao stores	Taobao crowdfunding requires that any crowdfunding initiator must open a store on Taobao before launching projects
c+ incubation project	On April 11, 2015, Taobao crowdfunding announced to launch "c + incubation plan", which is positioned to be the incubation platform of innovators and creativity, and will collect high tech products and design of the products with the biggest selling point around the world

Data Source www.yingcanzixun.com
[a]Blind order refers to a way of marketing and sales that buyers will prepay the specified price for a product without knowing the physical features and price of the product, only with the promise of the producer that what the buyers will receive should be worth more than what they pre-paid. http://baike.baidu.com/link?url=1gpzJCQCXAghkRxKPl0CuN3R8Htaes5XU-X-LHElZromuuxexbGc1yNsw1BRjTwEgUNQUpU7yr2sDh2A3yJCHihXZ3SzdJ_OXdIZ-9xr8RS

The headquarters of the platform is located in Shenzhen, and its website was launched in January 2014.[4] As a member of the first 8 equity crowdfunding pilot platforms of the Securities Association of China and one of the earliest director units of China's National Internet Finance Association, Zhongtoubang's primary focus was on equity financing for the projects with listing potentials through the model of "leading investor + following investor".

Zhongtoubang's business scope concentrates on the high-quality equity projects in some emerging industries, and all the leading investors of the financed projects are the top 200 professional investment institutions ranked by Zero2IPO. At present, Zhongtoubang continues to collaborate with a number of venture capitals, listed companies and local governments to jointly launch leading investment funds, buyout funds, as well as fund of funds (FoF) for industrial transformations.

5.4.2 The Performance of Zhongtoubang

All the projects posted on the Zhongtoubang platform are equity crowdfunding projects, with the highest financing amount for a single project up to RMB 50 million, and the lowest amount of RMB 10 million. By the end of September 2016, Zhongtoubang has accumulatively helped raise funds for nearly 50 projects through the equity crowdfunding, with accumulated investment amount of about RMB 1 billion. Currently, Zhongtoubang has 51,000 registered users and more than 8000 investors passing the Investors Qualification Assessment. In the first three quarters of 2016 alone, Zhongtoubang successfully raised the funds through equity crowdfunding for 12 projects, with RMB 161.53 million (Table 5.7).

5.4.3 Some Features of Zhongtoubang

See Table 5.8.

5.4.4 Profiting Model of Zhongtoubang Crowdfunding

Similar to other crowdfunding platforms, Zhongtoubang charges 3% of the total amount of the raised founds as the service fee.

[4]http://www.zhongtou8.cn/.

Table 5.7 The performance of Zhongtoubang: Q1–Q3 2016

The performance of Zhongtoubang: Q1–Q3 2016	
Total number of successful projects	12
Average project completion rate	97.1%
Annual amount of actually raised funds	RMB 161.53 Million
Number of investors	546

Data Source www.yingcanzixun.com

Table 5.8 The characteristics of Zhongtoubang

The characteristics of Zhongtoubang: recreate traditional venture capital investment with internet thinking	
Raising funds	Raising funds: to create the new model of "leading investment + following investment", help institutional investors enlarge fund leverage, and assist individual investors in investing in equity projects following institutional investors
Investment	Investment projects: to cultivate "crowd-innovating community", to provide customized training service for new investment managers, and excavate more "talent scouts" for the venture capital industry through fostering new prominent investment professionals
Management	Post-investment management: to provide diverse post-investment value-added services such as distribution channels, investor relations and conference activities for the projects
Exit	Project exit: installing a "safety lock" for "acquisition funds" and "fund of fund". Zhongtoubang ensures the successful investment and exit of investment by introducing multi-layer fund structure, such as fund of funds and acquisition funds

Data Source www.yingcanzixun.com

5.5 Dreammove Crowdfunding

5.5.1 The Developmental Performance of Dreammove Crowdfunding

Dreammove is a crowdfunding platform, with the headquarters located in Hangzhou, focusing on equity crowdfunding for new ventures through the internet.[5] The platform's website officially went online on October 28, 2014. As one of the top 100 enterprises that received the support from the Zhejiang Provincial Commission for Economy and Information in 2016, Dreammove Crowdfunding successfully conducted equity crowdfunding for 27 projects in the first three quarters of 2016, with the total raised amount up to RMB 47.965 million. The primary business model of the Dreammove is "leading investment + following investment" (Table 5.9).

[5]http://www.dreammove.cn/.

Table 5.9 The performance of Dreammove crowdfunding: Q1–Q3 2016

The performance of Dreammove: Q1–Q3 2016	
Total number of projects	27
Total amount of actually raised funds	RMB 47.965 million

Data Source www.yingcanzixun.com

Table 5.10 The characteristics of Dreammove crowdfunding

Characteristics of Dreammove crowdfunding	
Main focus	Dreammove mainly focuses on seed-round and angel-round projects and only conducts the first crowdfunding financing for primarily new entrepreneurial projects, as this type of projects have larger development potentials
Financing business	Dreammove provides financing service for project initiators and collect shares as returns, and the shares held are associated with the shares of crowdfunding to bind all parties' interests together, and allow the exit expectation with higher incomes
Creating ecosystem	On the basis of continuing improving the creation of entrepreneurial ecosystem and providing entrepreneurial incubator site, technology outsourcing and resource for entrepreneurial teams, Dreammove cooperate with some star enterprises of the industry to re-direct the resources to the platform, so as to attract outstanding talents and creativity to integrate these resources. At the same time, Dreammove raises the first time funds for these outstanding talents through crowdfunding. The first incubation project "waterfall technology" obtained successful crowdfunding and now entered into research and development stage
Building alliance	At the same time, Dreammove built up a crowdfunding platform alliance nationwide, aiming to creating a sharing ecology for the crowdfunding industry. At present, 12 crowdfunding platforms have gone online, which are located in Beijing, Shanghai, Guangzhou, Shenzhen, Zhejiang, Chengdu, Urumqi, Zhengzhou and Xiamen. The other cooperative platforms are under negotiation, which will go online subsequently in the future

Data Source www.yingcanzixun.com

5.5.2 The Characteristics of Dreammove Crowdfunding

See Table 5.10.

5.5.3 The Profiting Model of Dreammove Crowdfunding

Following the main stream, Dreammove charges 3–5% of the actual raised amount as service fee for all equity crowdfunding projects on Dreammove platform, if the financing succeeds.

Chapter 6
The Policies and Regulations of Crowdfunding Industry

Zhi Chen, Haimei Wang and Lixiu Gao

Since 2015, the financial regulators in China have recognized the importance of inclusive finance provided by internet finance, and encouraged an orderly and healthy development of the industry. With the occurrence of several incidents, such as eZubao and Kuailuxi, however, the regulators also began to take actions to rectify the internet finance industry and crack down the illegal fundraising activities. From 2015 to September 2016, the regulators have issued a series of policies, aiming at standardizing the growth of the internet financial industry including crowdfunding.

6.1 The Instructions of Government on Crowdfunding Industry

On March 5, 2016, Premier Li Keqiang delivered his annual state of country report at the Fourth Session of the Twelfth National People's Congress. The report strongly encouraged the entrepreneurship, innovation and wide applications of internet, known as "Internet +", and proposed to establish the integrated platforms that support massive involvement of general public and crowdfunding from a wide spectrum of participants, and a new mechanism that can effectively coordinate all the efforts of the enterprises of all scales, colleges and universities, research institutions, and individuals in the market.[1]

[1]National Internet Finance Association of China, March 07, 2016, http://www.isc.org.cn/zxzx/ywsd/listinfo-33305.html.

Z. Chen (✉) · H. Wang · L. Gao
Shanghai Wenxi Investment Consulting Co., Shanghai, China
e-mail: chenzhi@wdzj.com

J.G. Wang et al. (eds.), *Financing from Masses*,
https://doi.org/10.1007/978-981-10-5843-1_6

On March 18, 2016, Shenzhen Internet Finance Association issued the Notice on Prohibition of Speculative Crowdfunding in the Real Estate Industry and Control of Financial Risks, requiring all Shenzhen internet financial firms to stop financing activities in the "bubbled" real estate market through crowdfunding, conduct self-examinations, and take correction actions.[2]

On April 14, 2016, the State Council organized 14 ministries and commissions to hold a TV conference, and announced an one-year special rectification plan in the internet finance industry nationwide. On the same day, the State Council approved and issued the documentations related with the proposed rectification. The rectification involves in seven sub-plans and multiple ministries and commissions of the state council. Among them, the People's Bank of China, China Banking Regulatory Commission (CBRC), China Security Regulatory Commission (CSRC) and China Insurance Regulatory Commission (CIRC) will issue special rectification rules in their respective fields, such as online payment, peer-to-peer lending, equity crowdfunding and internet insurance, and some ministries or commissions are responsible for more than one rectification sub-plans.[3]

On April 21, 2016, Guangzhou Association of Financial Industry, Guangzhou Internet Finance Association and Guangzhou Real Estate Agents Association jointly issued the Notice on Prohibition of Down Payment Loan and Speculative Crowdfunding in Real Estate Market, requiring all members of these organizations to stop the down payment loans and crowdfunding for real estate property purchases, conduct self-examinations, and take correction actions.[4]

On April 27, 2016, 14 ministries and commissions of the State Council including the People's Bank of China, CSRC, CIRC, CBRC, the Supreme People's Procuratorate, the Ministry of Industry and Information Technology, and the Ministry of Public Safety convened an Inter-ministerial Meeting on the illegal fundraising activities to report the current status of the illegal fundraising activities and adopt the resolutions on resolving these issues. In particular, the CSRC will be responsible in six areas, including illegal issuance of the original stock shares, special examination of internet-based equity financing platforms, and further standardization of private equity fund governance. At the meeting, the CSRC expressed its intention to amend the current Securities Law by standardizing and regulating the equity crowdfunding and private equity financing.[5]

On May 27, 2016, the National Small-and-Medium-Sized Enterprise Share Transfer System published the Notice on Financial Enterprises' Listing and Financing. The Notice categorized all financial companies by the enterprises regulated by "One Bank and Three Commissions", private equity institutions and other financial enterprises, and specified that the System will, temporarily, not accept the

[2]Eastmoney, March 21, 2016, http://finance.eastmoney.com/news/1345,20160321606151686.html.

[3]Online Lending House, April 16, 2016, http://www.wdzj.com/news/hangye/28079.html.

[4]Online Lending House, April 16, 2016, http://www.wdzj.com/news/zhengce/28236.html.

[5]Online Lending House, April 28, 2016, http://www.wdzj.com/news/zhengce/28438.html.

listing applications from the companies in the "other financial enterprises" category before the relevant regulations are in place. For the enterprises applying for listing that do not belong to "other financial enterprises" category but possess more than 20% (including 20%) of shares of "other financial enterprises" or are the largest shareholders of these firms, their listing applications will not be accepted temporarily, either. For these already accepted applications, the reviews will be terminated immediately.[6]

6.2 The Regulations and Policies of Crowdfunding Industry

2015 is widely considered the "Year One of Regulation" for the internet financial industry in China. From 2015 to the end of September 2016, the central government has issued a series of policy announcements on encouraging the development of crowdfunding and non-public equity financing, such as "The Guidance on Developing Massive Innovation and Entrepreneurship", "The Opinions of the State Council on Actively Promoting "Internet +" Activities", "The Notice of the State Council on the Development Plan of Inclusive Finance (2016–2020)", as well as "The Outline of the Thirteenth Five-Year Plan for National Economic and Social Development". At the same time, the central government also issued a series of special rectification schemes for internet finance industry, including "The Opinions of the State Council on Preventing Illegal Fundraising" and "The Notice of the State Administration for Industry and Commerce on 2016 Special Rectifications for Internet Market". It appears that China's central government took a stance that strictly cracks down the illegal fundraising activities while totally encourages and supports the development of crowdfunding. At the same time, the government also urges the regulatory agencies to timely issue the relevant policies to standardize the operation of equity crowdfunding and guide the healthy and orderly development of the industry (Table 6.1).

6.3 Local Regulatory Policies of Crowdfunding Industry

As the crowdfunding industry developed rapidly with progressively issued regulatory policies from central government agencies, some local governments also actively responded to the requirements from the regulators of the central government and market to issue some related policies focusing on the specific geographical areas. Fox example, the local governments in some faster developed

[6]National Small-and-Medium-Sized Enterprise Share Transfer System: Notice on Financial Enterprises' Listing and Financing, Equity System Announcement, 2016, No. 36.

Table 6.1 Regulations and policies for crowdfunding industry: 2015–September 2016

Time	Law	Issuing agency	Specific content
March 2015	Guiding Opinions on Developing Crowd-Innovating Space and Promoting Massive Innovation and Ventures[a]	General Office of the State Council	Exert the function of multi-level capital market, and provide comprehensive financial services for innovative enterprises; carry out internet-based equity crowdfunding pilots, and increase the serving capability of crowdfunding to massive innovation and venture; standardize and develop regional equity market serving micro and small enterprises, promote new scientific and technological ventures, and improve the exit and circulation mechanism of angel investment
July 2015	Guiding Opinions of the State Council on Actively Promoting "Internet +" Action[b]	The State Council	Actively exert the leading function of angel investment and venture capital for "Internet +". Carry out Internet finance innovation pilots, such as equity crowdfunding pilots, to support the development of micro and small enterprises; carry out innovation pilots in integration of industry and finance, and explore new financing services by combining equity and debt financing
July 2015	Guiding Opinions on Promoting the Healthy Development of Internet Finance	Ten ministries and commissions including the People's Bank of China	Equity crowdfunding needs to be conducted through the platforms of equity crowdfunding of intermediary institutions (internet websites or other similar electronic media). On the premise of abiding by laws and regulations, equity crowdfunding intermediary institutions can make innovative exploration on business models, exert the function

(continued)

Table 6.1 (continued)

Time	Law	Issuing agency	Specific content
			of equity crowdfunding as the integrated part of multi-level capital market and serve innovating and venture enterprises in a better way. Equity crowdfunding business is regulated by the CSRC
August 2015	Notice on Conducting Special Examination for the Institutions Carrying out Equity Financing Activities via the Internet	China Securities Regulatory Commission (CSRC)	Without the approval of securities regulatory agencies of State Council, any entity or individual shall not conduct equity crowdfunding activities. At present, some "equity crowdfunding" activities conducted by some entities in the market is indeed conducting non-public equity financing or privately raising equity funds via the Internet, which is beyond the scope of equity crowdfunding specified in the guiding opinions
September 2015	Guiding Opinions on Accelerating the Construction of the Platforms to Support Massive Innovation and Entrepreneurship[c]	State Council	Encourage innovative products, such as consumer electronics, intelligent household products, health devices and special agricultural products, to conduct physical product crowdfunding. Support creative projects including art, publishing and film and television projects to carry out physical product crowdfunding with strengthened content management. Stably promote equity crowdfunding pilot projects, and encourage micro-and-small enterprises and entrepreneurs to raise the early stage equity through the model of equity crowdfunding

(continued)

Table 6.1 (continued)

Time	Law	Issuing agency	Specific content
September 2015	Opinions on Promoting Online and Offline Interaction and Accelerating the Innovative Development and Transformation and Upgrading of Businesses[d]	General Office of the State Council	Strengthen support in finance, O2O (online and offline interactive) enterprises at different development stages, third-party payment, and non-public equity financing
October 2015	Opinions on Accelerating the Innovative Development of Online and Offline Integration of Service Industry[e]	Ministry of Commerce	All local commercial departments shall appropriately use the special funds from central government for the development of financial service industry. Direct enterprises in service industry to fully utilize the multi-level capital market, and obtain financial resources for innovation through Internet-based non-public equity financing. Conduct research and issue policies on establishing inter-enterprise system, inter-industry interactive system and cross-field coordination system
December 2015	Opinions on Further Improvement of the Ratio of Direct Financing and Optimizing Financial Structure	State Council	Lowering down the financing cost for real sectors of Chinese economy; reducing the leverage ratio of Chinese companies; and diversifying the risks of China's financial system
January 2016	Notice of the State Council on Development of Planning for Promoting Inclusive Finance (2016–2020)[f]	State Council	Actively encourage online payment institutions to serve e-business development, provide small-amount, fast and convenient payment services for the society and improve payment efficiency; Taking advantages of convenience and wide coverage of customer segments, help alleviate the difficulties in

(continued)

Table 6.1 (continued)

Time	Law	Issuing agency	Specific content
			financing for micro and small enterprises, farmers and various low-income consumers; Exert the supporting function of equity crowdfunding platforms on massive innovation and entrepreneurship; Establish various types of laws and regulations on inclusive financial service; Amend the Securities Law and consolidate the legal foundation of equity crowdfunding
February 2016	Opinions of the State Council on Further Preventing and Disposing Illegal Financing	State Council	Accelerate the setup of laws and regulations on private financing and new forms of financing activities; Issue organizational rules on non-deposit type of loans as soon as possible, regulate private financing market participants and expand legal financing channels; Issue regulatory rules on P2P lending and equity crowdfunding as soon as possible, and promote the standardized development of Internet finance; Thoroughly research and standardize the policies and measures on wealth management, non-financing guarantee and other financial activities conducted by private financial intermediaries, and timely issue the relevant policies that are consistent with business reforms
March 2016	Outline of the Thirteenth Five-year Plan for National Economic and Social Development	The Fourth Session of the Twelfth National People's Congress	Rely on the Internet to expand the channels to connect market resources and social demands with entrepreneurial innovation.

(continued)

Table 6.1 (continued)

Time	Law	Issuing agency	Specific content
			Promote professional development, online platforms and internal crowd-innovation of enterprises, and strengthen sharing of innovation resources. Promote creativity, manufacturing operation and maintenance, knowledge content and service, propel the public to participate in online production and circulation; Develop public crowd-support, sharing crowd-support and interactive crowd-support; Improve the regulation system, and standardize the development of reward crowdfunding, equity crowdfunding and P2P online lending
April 2016	Notice of the State Council on Issuing the Scheme for Promoting Comprehensive and Innovative Reform and Accelerating the Construction of Global Scientific and Technological Innovation Center[g]	State Council	Support Shanghai Equity Exchange to set up a special board of scientific and technological innovation; Support Shanghai to conduct equity crowdfunding pilot projects
May 2016	Notice of the State Administration for Industry and Commerce on Issuing 2016 Special Action Plan for Regulating Network Market[h]	State Administration for Industry and Commerce	All local Administration for Industry and Commerce and Market Regulation Department should strictly implement the provisions of the Advertisement Law, strengthen research on socially focused and difficult issues, strictly regulate and control Internet advertisement market; Further strengthen supervision, and strictly crack down false and illegal Internet advertisements; Fully exert the function of the joint-ministerial

(continued)

Table 6.1 (continued)

Time	Law	Issuing agency	Specific content
			meeting for rectifying false and illegal advertisements, strengthen coordination and communication, information sharing and law enforcement cooperation between departments, and carry out special rectification on Internet financial advertisements
August 2016	The Thirteenth-five Plan for National Scientific and Technological Innovation[i]	The State Council	Strengthen comprehensive carrier construction of innovation and venture, develop crowd-innovating space, and support the transformation and upgrading of service economy, such as crowd-innovating, crowd-contracting, crowd-supporting and crowd-raising; exert the important promoting effect of financial innovation on innovation and venture, develop financial products and service that comply with innovation needs, and make efforts to develop venture capital and multi-level capital market, improve the mechanism of combining science and technology and finance, and improve the ratio of direct finance; promote intellectual property securitization pilots and equity crowdfunding financing pilots, explore and standardize the development of Internet finance with innovative service

(continued)

Table 6.1 (continued)

Time	Law	Issuing agency	Specific content
September 2016	Some Opinions on Promoting the Healthy Development of Venture Capital	State Council	Actively encourage various types of individuals including angel investors to be engaged in venture capital investments; Encourage the establishment of all types of platforms and organizations including non-profit angel investor alliance, cultivate and develop angel investor group, promote communication and cooperation among angel investors, new ventures and venture capital enterprises, create healthy angel investment environment, and promote the development of angel investment industry; Standardize the development of Internet-based equity financing platforms and provide information and technology services for individuals to directly invest in new ventures

Data Source www.yingcanzixun.com

[a]General Office of the State Council, The Guidance on Developing Massive Innovation and Entrepreneurship, GBF (2015) No. 9

[b]State Council, The Opinions of the State Council on Actively Promoting "Internet +" Activities, GF (2015) No. 40

[c]State Council, Guiding Opinions about Accelerating the Construction of Massive Innovation and Entrepreneurship Supporting Platform, GF (2015) No. 53

[d]State Council, Opinions on Promoting Online and Offline Interaction and Accelerating the Innovative Development and Transformation of Commercial Activities, GBF (2015) No. 72

[e]Ministry of Commerce, Opinions on Accelerating the Innovative Development of Online and Offline Integration of Service Industry, SFMH (2015) No. 865

[f]State Council, Notice on Issuing the Development Plan for Promoting Inclusive Finance (2016–2020), GF (2015) No. 74

[g]State Council, Notice on Issuing the Scheme for Promoting Comprehensive Innovation and Accelerating the Construction of Global Scientific and Technological Innovation Center, GF (2015) No. 23

[h]State Administration for Industry and Commerce, Notice on Issuing 2016 Special Action Plan for Regulating Network Market, GSBZI (2016) No. 7

[i]State Council, Notice on Issuance of the Thirteenth-Five Plan for National Scientific and Technological Innovations, GF (2016) No. 43

Table 6.2 Local regulatory policies of crowdfunding industry: 2015–September 2016

Time	Name	Issuing agency
January 2015	Opinions of Guangzhou Government on Implementation of Promoting the Development of Internet Finance Industry[a]	General Office of Guangzhou Municipal People's Government
May 2015	Some Opinions on Implementation of the State Administration for Industry and Commerce Supporting the Construction of Guangdong Free Trade Pilot Zone[b]	Guangdong Provincial Administration for Industry and Commerce
June 2015	Some Opinions on Supporting the Development of Crowd-innovating Space of Shanghai[c]	Shanghai Municipal Administration for Industry and Commerce
July 2015	Some Opinions on Improving the Investment and Financing Mechanism of Micro and Small Enterprises in an Innovative way[d]	Guangdong Provincial Government
July 2015	Working Scheme for Guangdong Carrying out Internet-based Equity Crowdfunding Pilots[e]	Guangdong Finance Office
August 2015	Opinions on Conducting Internet Equity Crowdfunding Pilots of Shandong Province[f]	Shandong Finance Office
September 2015	"Internet +" Action Plan of Guangdong Province (2015–2020)[g]	Guangdong Provincial Government
September 2015	Opinions on Promoting the Accelerated Development of Service Industry[h]	Jinan Municipal Government
October 2015	Opinions on Vigorously Promoting Massive Innovation and Entrepreneurship[i]	Beijing Municipal Government
October 2015	Opinions on Fully Utilizing Multi-level Capital Market, Adjusting Industrial Structure, Changing Ways of Development and Upgrading Industries[j]	Anhui Provincial Government
October 2015	Opinions on Accelerating the Development of Multi-level Capital Market of Shanxi Province[k]	General Office of Shanxi Provincial Government
October 2015	Implementation Scheme of Hunan Province for Developing Crowd-innovating Space and Promoting Massive Innovation and Entrepreneurship[l]	Human Province
November 2015	Opinions on Financially Supporting the Construction of (Tianjin) Free Trade Zone (Tianjin Free Trade Zone, Finance Reform, Clause 33)[m]	Tianjin Municipal Government

(continued)

Table 6.2 (continued)

Time	Name	Issuing agency
January 2016	Opinions of Beijing Municipal People's Government on Actively Promoting "Internet +" Action[n]	General Office of Beijing Municipal People's Government
January 2016	"Internet +" Action Plan of Zhejiang Province[o]	Zhejiang Provincial People's Government
February 2016	Opinions on Implementation of "Internet +" Action[p]	Shanghai Municipal People's Government
February 2016	Some Opinions of the General Office of Jiangxi Provincial People's Government on Promoting the Development of Internet Finance[q]	General Office of Jiangxi Provincial People's Government
February 2016	Measures of Management on Further Preventing and Disposing Illegal Fundraising[r]	General Office of Beijing Municipal People's Government
February 2016	2016 Priority of Shaanxi Provincial Party Committee's Science and Technology Working Committee and Shaanxi Provincial Science and Technology Department[s]	Shaanxi Provincial Party Committee Science and Technology Working Committee of CPC and Shaanxi Provincial Science and Technology Department
March 2016	Working System of Guangdong Province for Monitoring and Early Warning of Illegal Fund-raising[t]	Guangdong Provincial Finance Office
March 2016	Opinions of Guangzhou Municipal People's Government on Further Preventing and Disposing Illegal Fundraising Activities[u]	General Office of Guangzhou Municipal People's Government
April 2016	Opinions on Preventing and Disposing Illegal Fundraising[v]	Shanghai Municipal People's Government
April 2016	Notice of Guangzhou Municipal Financial Bureau on Special Rectification on Risk Prevention of Equity Investment Enterprises[w]	Guangzhou Municipal Financial Bureau
May 2016	Scheme for Implementing Special Rectification on Internet Financial Risks[x]	General Office of Erdos Municipal People's Government
June 2016	Scheme of Fujian Province for Special Rectification on Internet Financial Risks[y]	General Office of Fujian Provincial People's Government
June 2016	"Internet +" Action Plan of Shandong Province (2016–2018)[z]	Shandong Provincial People's Government
July 2016	Notice on Further Supporting Migrant-workers in Starting Business in Hometowns[aa]	Guangdong Provincial People's Government

Data Source www.yingcanzixun.com

[a]General Office of Guangzhou Municipal People's Government, Opinions of Guangzhou on Promoting the Development of Internet Finance Industry, SFB (2015) No. 3

[b]Guangdong Provincial Administration for Industry and Commerce, Some Opinions of the State Administration for Industry and Commerce on Supporting the Construction of Guangdong Free Trade Pilot Zone. July 10, 2015, http://zwgk.gd.gov.cn/00694001X/201507/t20150710_590190.html
[c]Shanghai Municipal Administration for Industry and Commerce, Some Opinions of Shanghai Municipal Administration for Industry and Commerce on Supporting the Development of Crowd-innovating Space of Shanghai, HGSZ (2015) No. 126
[d]Guangdong Provincial People's Government, Some Opinions on Innovatively Improving the Investment and Financing Mechanism of Micro and Small Enterprises, YF (2015) No. 66
[e]Guangdong Finance Office, Working Scheme for Guangdong Conducting Internet Equity Crowdfunding Pilots, YJ (2015) No. 46
[f]Shandong Finance Office, Opinions on Conducing Internet-based Equity Crowdfunding Pilots. August 26, 2015, http://www.sdjrb.gov.cn/art/2015/08/26/art_11270_334989.html
[g]General Office of Guangdong Provincial Government, Notice on Issuing the "Internet +" Action Plan of Guangdong Province (2015–2020), YFB (2015) No. 53
[h]Jinan Municipal People's Government, Opinions on the Accelerated Development of Service Industry, JZF (2015) No. 16
[i]Beijing Municipal People's Government, Opinions on Vigorous Promotion of Massive Innovation and Entrepreneurship, JZF (2015) No. 49
[j]Anhui Provincial People's Government, Opinions on Fully Utilizing Multi-level Capital Market, Adjusting Industrial Structure, Changing Ways of Development, and Promoting Upgrading Industries, WZ (2015) No. 90
[k]General Office of Shanxi Provincial Government, Opinions on Development of Multi-level Capital Market of Shandong Province, JZBF (2015) No. 90
[l]General Office of Human Provincial People's Government, Notice on Scheme of Hunan Province for Developing Crowd-innovating Space and Promoting Massive Innovation and Entrepreneurship, XZBF (2015) No. 74
[m]People's Bank of China, Guiding Opinions on Financially Supporting the Construction of China (Tianjin) Free Trade Zone. December 11, 2015, http://www.pbc.gov.cn/goutongjiaoliu/113456/113469/2988345/index.html
[n]Beijing Municipal People's Government, Opinions on Actively Promoting "Internet +" Action, JZF (2016) No. 4
[o]Zhejiang Provincial People's Government, Notice on Issuing the "Internet +" Action Plan of Zhejiang Province. January 28, 2016, http://www.jingning.gov.cn/art/2016/1/28/art_3913_260080.html
[p]Shanghai Municipal People's Government, Notice on Issuing the Opinions of Shanghai on Promoting "Internet +" Action, HFF (2016) No. 9
[q]General Office of Jiangxi Provincial People's Government, Some Opinions on Development of Internet Finance of the Province, GFTF (2016) No. 3
[r]General Office of Beijing Municipal People's Government, Notice on Issuing the Measures of Management of Further Preventing and Disposing Illegal Fund-raising, JZBF (2016) No. 2
[s]Shaanxi Provincial Science and Technology Department, 2016 Priorities of Science and Technology Working Committee of CPC and Shaanxi Provincial Science and Technology Department, February, 26, 2016, http://www.shaanxi.gov.cn/0/1/11/3753/209059.htm
[t]Finance Office of Guangdong Provincial People's Government, Notice on the Working System of Guangdong Province for Monitoring and Early Warning of Illegal Fund-raising, March 15, 2016, http://zwgk.gd.gov.cn/759214127/201603/t20160330_649786.html
[u]Guangzhou Municipal People's Government, Opinions on Further Preventing and Disposing Illegal Fund-raising, SFH (2016) No. 48
[v]Shanghai Municipal People's Government, Notice on Issuing the Opinions on Preventing and Disposing Illegal Fund-raising, HFF (2015) No. 19

[w]Guangzhou Municipal Financial Bureau, Notice of Guangzhou Municipal Financial Bureau on Special Rectification on Risk Prevention of Equity Investment Enterprises, April 22, 2016, http://www.gzjr.gov.cn/gzjr/tzgg/201604/d6513fe7bff149c8b36be3daecc28274.shtml
[x]General Office of Ordos Municipal People's Government, Notice on Issuing the Scheme for Implementing Special Rectification on Internet Financial Risks, EFBFD (2016) No. 17
[y]General Office of Fujian Provincial People's Government, Notice on Issuing the Scheme of Fujian Province for Special Rectification on Internet Financial Risks, MZB (2016) No. 76
[z]Shandong Provincial People's Government, Notice on Issuing the "Internet +" Action Plan of Shandong Province (2016–2018), LZF (2016) No. 14
[aa]General Office of Guangdong Provincial People's Government, Notice on Further Supporting Migrant-Workers in Starting Business in Hometowns, YFB (2016) No. 68

areas, such as Beijing, Shanghai and Guangdong, have issued some localized supporting policies for crowdfunding industry, including "The Opinions of Guangzhou Municipal Government on Implementation and Promotion of the Development of Internet Finance Industry", "The Opinions of Beijing Municipal Government on Implementation and Promotion of "Internet +" Activities" and "The Opinions of Shanghai Municipal Government on Promoting "Internet +" Programs", as well as some policies regulating non-public equity financing, such as "The Measures of Beijing Municipal Government on Preventing Illegal Fundraising", as summarized in Table 6.2. In addition, the local government in the central and western regions in China also set up some localized regulatory policies, such as "Opinions of Jiangxi Provincial Government on Promoting the Development of Internet Finance Industry of the Jiangxi Province", and "2016 Key Focuses of Shaanxi Provincial Science & Technology Commission and Shaanxi Provincial Science and Technology Department". It can be seen from these local regulatory policies issued from 2015 to September 2016, the local regulators, not only in these developed areas such as Beijing, Shanghai and Guangdong, but also the central and western regions, all attempted to keep pace with the central government on cracking down the illegal fundraising activities and rectifying the non-public equity financing while encouraging the development of crowdfunding industry in a healthy and orderly way.

Chapter 7
Financing Status of China's Crowdfunding Platforms

Zhi Chen and Haimei Wang

From January 2016 to September 2016, 12 crowdfunding platforms obtained venture capital investment in China, including Dreammove, Zhongchouke, Xingfami, Xingchou, WeiCi Finance, Huimeng Zone, Yingdaren, Fun in Funding, Jingbei Crowdfunding, Kaistart Crowdfunding, Duocaitou and Yimi Haodi. Among them, Kaistart Crowdfunding completed two rounds of financing in 2016.

- **Kaistart Crowdfunding's Twice Financing in the First Three Quarters in 2016**

Kaistart Crowdfunding is a crowdfunding platform focusing on the new life style consumption projects with both physical products and consumption experience as the returns for the investors. On February 2, Kaistart Crowdfunding announced its access to an A+ round financing with Matrix Partners and Yuanjing Capital as the investors, even though the investment amount is not released.[1] On June 16, Kaistart Crowdfunding announced its completion of the B-round financing of RMB 100 million, with Kunlun Wanwei as the leading investor, Daosen Capital and Qingsong Capital as the following investors, and four existing shareholders, including Yuanjing Capital, Matrix Partners, Yinbaodian Capital and In Capital, increasing their holdings of the Kaistart. As it was circulated in the crowdfunding community, Kaistart obtained angel capital from In Capital in April 2015, and A-round investment of RMB 33.5 million from Meridian Capital and Yinbaodian Capital in November 2015.

[1]http://36kr.com/p/5048170.html.

Z. Chen (✉) · H. Wang
Shanghai Wenxi Investment Consulting Co., Shanghai, China
e-mail: chenzhi@wdzj.com

J.G. Wang et al. (eds.), *Financing from Masses*,
https://doi.org/10.1007/978-981-10-5843-1_7

- **Dreammove Received 10-Million-Level A-Round Financing**

Dreammove is a service platform that helps start-ups to obtain non-public equity financing through the internet. At the end of February 2016, Dreammove announced its access to a 10-million-level A-round financing with the firm valuation of RMB 150 million.[2] The inflow of the capital is jointly invested by Dingju Capital, Yu Pi, the founder of Dapeng Capital, as well as Li Zhiguo, the chairman and CEO of Dig Fortune.

- **Zhongchouke Obtained 10-Million-Level A-Round Investment**

As a subsidiary of Beijing Zhongchouke Network Technology Co., Ltd., Zhongchouke is a crowdfunding platform focusing on the city-wide physical chain stores providing catering and entertainment services. Zhongchouke obtained angel investment nearly RMB 10 million from multiple institutions and individuals, including KRC Investment and the famous angel investor Song Yuhai, in July 2015. On March 23, Zhongchouke announced its access to a 10-million-level A-round financing, with Neo Capital as the leading investor and multiple existing individual shareholders as the following investors.[3]

- **Xingfami Acquired Strategic Investment of RMB 3 Million**

Xingfami, a subsidiary of Fami (Shenzhen) Internet Finance Co., Ltd., is a crowdfunding platform focusing on used cars transactions, and went online on April 18, 2015. At the very early stage of its development, its primary business was the pledged loans, but it shifted its core business line to used cars crowdfunding later. In April 2016, Xingfami announced its obtaining a strategic investment of RMB 3 million from some well-known investors.[4]

- **Taoyuji Completed Its Angel-Round Financing**

Taoyuji (formerly known as Xingchou) is an internet-based crowdfunding platform specialized in the vertical sub-fields of cultural entertainment industry. At present, its primary business is to take movies online, and started its operation in November 2015. As it is circulated in the internet finance community, Taoyuji completed its angel-round financing at the end of April 2016, with the funds invested by Suhehui.[5]

- **WeiCi Received 10-Million-Level Pre-A-Round Financing**

WeiCi Finance is a crowdfunding platform focusing on used car crowdfunding project at present. It received several millions of angel-round investment in July 2015, and the investor was Xinjin Capital. On May 3, 2016, WeiCi Finance announced its completion of a 10-million-level Pre-A round financing, with Gobi

---

[2]Dreammove, http://www.dreammove.cn/static/about/key/newtrends.html.

[3]http://business.sohu.com/20160323/n441656644.shtml.

[4]http://money.163.com/16/0419/17/BL1IA64E00253B0H.html.

[5]http://www.258.com/news/1403083.html.

Partners as the leading investor, and Rushan Investments and Fenghou Capital as the following investors.[6]

- **Huimeng Zone Obtained Pre-A-Round Financing of RMB 15 Million**

Huimeng Zone is a crowdfunding platform focusing on catering industry, and officially went online in June 2015. On May 12, 2016, Huimeng Zone announced publicly its access to a Pre-A-round financing of RMB 15 million, with Qiantong Capital as the leading investor and several professional investors as the following investors.[7]

- **Yingdaren Accessed to an Angel-Round Financing of RMB 2 Million**

Officially going online in December 2015, Yingdaren is a film and television crowdfunding platform focusing on online movies, and uses equity earning right as the way of return for the investors. At the end of May 2016, Yingdaren announced its access to an angel-round financing of RMB 2 million from Chuangmeng Investments.[8]

- **Fun in Funding Received B+ Round Financing of Nearly RMB 20 Million**

Fun in Funding is a crowdfunding platform focusing on social network field, and went online on August 12, 2014. About four month later, Fun in Funding was reported to obtain several millions of A-round investment from IDG on December 7, 2014, A+ round investment from Wu Bin, the founder and director of Vipshop, on April 15 2015, and a 10-million-level B-round investment from DT Capital Partners and IDG Capital on December 12, 2015. On June 1, 2016, Fun in Funding announced that it had completed a B+ round financing of nearly RMB 20 million, jointly invested by Tencent, IDG, DT Capital Partners, and Tongdao Capital.[9]

- **Jingbei Finance and Jingbei Crowdfunding Received A-Round Financing of RMB 30 Million**

As a subsidiary of Jingbei Finance, Jingbei Crowdfunding is an equity crowdfunding platform, adopting the model of "leading investment + following investment", and primarily covering the fields of new finance, new services, new consumption, and new business of real sectors. On June 6, Jingbei Finance and Jingbei Crowdfunding announced its access to an A-round financing of RMB 30 million from Lakala Internet Finance Group.[10]

---

[6]http://money.163.com/16/0503/11/BM4U7J4500253B0H.html.

[7]http://www.chinaz.com/news/2016/0512/530678.shtml.

[8]http://mi.chinabyte.com/39/13800539.shtml.

[9]http://36kr.com/p/5047664.html.

[10]http://news.sina.com.cn/o/2016-06-16/doc-ifxtfmrp2102933.shtml.

- **Duocaitou Accessed to 10-Million-Level Pre-A Round Financing**

Duocaitou is a crowdfunding platform focusing on the field of boutique hotel and accommodations, adopting a "spatial crowdfunding model" of "PE + crowdfunding". On August 8, 2016, Duocaitou announced its completion of a

Table 7.1 Financing status of crowdfunding platforms: January–September 2016

Platform	Financing time	Round	Investor	Financing amount
Kaistart Crowdfunding	February	A+ round	Matrix Partners and Yuanjing Capital	Not published
Dreammove	February	A round	Dingju Capital, Yu Pi, the founder of Dapeng Capital, as well as Li Zhiguo, the chairman and CEO of Dig Fortune	Ten-million level
Zhougchouke	March	A round	Neo capital leads investment and multiple individual shareholders follow the investment	Ten-million level
Xingfami	April	Angel round	Well-known investors	RMB 3 million
Taoyuji (formerly known as Xingchou)	April	Angel round	Suhehui	RMB 4 million
WeiCi Finance	May	Pre-A round	Gobi Partners leads investment, and Rushan Investments and Fenghou Capital follow the investment	Ten-million level
Huimeng Zone	May	Pre-A round	Qiantong Capital leads investment and professional investors follow the investment	RMB 15 million
Yingdaren	May	Angel round	Chuangmeng Investments	RMB 2 million
Fun in Funding	June	B+ round	Tencent, IDG, DT Capital Partners and Tongdao Capital	Nearly RMB 20 million
Jingbei Crowdfunding	June	A round	Lakala Internet Finance Group	RMB 30 million
Kaistart Crowdfunding	June	B round	Four old shareholders including Kunlun Wanwei, Yuanjing Capital, Matrix Partners, Yinbaodian Capital and In Capital lead investment, and Daosen Capital and Qingsong Capital participate in following investment	RMB 100 million
Duocaitou	August	Pre-A round	Innovation Angel Funds, Share Capital and Shuiwei Capital	Ten-million level
Yimi Haodi	August	A round	Zhongnan Capital	RMB 100 million

Data Source www.yingcanzixun.com

10-million-level Pre-A-round investment from Innovation Angel Funds, Share Capital, and Shuiwei Capital.[11]

- **Yimi Haodi Obtained A-Round Financing of RMB 100 Million**

Yimi Haodi is a real estate crowdfunding platform focusing on design and renovation of old houses and new high-end housing properties. Yimi Haodi once accessed to an angel-round investment in March 2015, and obtained a Pre-A-round financing from Triumph Capital in November 2015. On August 16, Yimi Haodi announced its access to an A-round financing of RMB 100 million from Zhongnan Capital (Table 7.1).[12]

[11]http://mt.sohu.com/20160808/n463143655.shtml.

[12]http://www.yimihaodi.com/news/detail-129.aspx.

Chapter 8
The Future Development of Crowdfunding Industry in China

Yexia Zhang and Zhi Chen

Crowdfunding industry was still in its rapid growth stage in 2016, in terms of either the number of operating platforms or the number of participating investors. Several sub-industries, such as used cars, agricultural products, and catering were observed fast growth during the year, while some other sub-industries, such as real estate, were seen to decline due to the restrictions of governmental policies. In 2016, the directions of future regulations for crowdfunding industry has gradually become clearer for general public. The regulators were taking non-public equity financing as the key rectification target, by issuing "The Scheme for Special Rectifications on Risk of Internet Finance", while still encouraging and supporting the overall development of crowdfunding industry, in the hope of fostering a market with standardized regulations and healthy development. As a result, the future development of crowdfunding industry can be expected to take in the following ways.

8.1 Integration and Standardization with Stricter Regulations

2016 will be undoubtedly labeled as the "Year of Compliance" or "Year of Regulation" for the internet finance industry in China. As the one-year-long special rectification on internet finance market was launched nationwide, the crowdfunding industry stepped into the stage of integration and standardization without options. The regulators took the non-public equity financing as the primary rectification target and set up some boundaries for this type of crowdfunding platforms, such as prohibitions of false bids, raising funds for the platforms themselves, issuance of debt financing in the name of equity financing, or conducting illegal fundraising

Y. Zhang (✉) · Z. Chen
Shanghai Wenxi Investment Consulting Co., Shanghai, China
e-mail: zhangyx@wdzj.com

J.G. Wang et al. (eds.), *Financing from Masses*,
https://doi.org/10.1007/978-981-10-5843-1_8

activities. As the rectification of internet finance will continue in 2017, some existing crowdfunding platforms can be projected to either operate in a more effective way of compliance with the announced policies or just simply exit from the industry. As a result, a more integrated and standardized crowdfunding industry can be reasonably expected. In particular, with the issuance of the Charity Law, the future charity crowdfunding platforms could be separated by two types—emergency assistance crowdfunding and charity crowdfunding. As the emergency assistance crowdfunding will not be regulated by any specific laws, the investors of emergency assistance crowdfunding have to make their decisions based on their own judgment and bear any possible risk and costs by themselves, if any incident incurred. The charity crowdfunding, on the other hand, needs to be operated in compliance with the Charity Law, so the possibility of fake or illegal projects that will be listed on the charity crowdfunding platforms will be projected to be much lower than that on emergency assistance crowdfunding platforms.

8.2 Accelerated Entry of Venture Capital

The rapid growth of the crowdfunding industry also attracted attention and entry of venture capitals into this emerging market, as evidenced by the statistics of the financing of the crowdfunding platforms in the first three quarters of 2016, as reported in this book. There were 12 crowdfunding platforms that received venture capital investment, and the investors included some well-known venture capitals, such as Tencent and Lakala. As the crowdfunding industry continues its innovation and growth, the accelerated entry of venture capital should be reasonably expected.

8.3 Specialization and Refinement

With the entry of internet giants such as JD, Taobao, Suning, 360, and Xiaomi, it would be difficult for small-and-medium-sized crowdfunding platforms to compete with these giant companies with rich resources and funds, and it becomes necessary for these smaller players to re-position themselves as a niche player in this re-structured market. It can be expected that more and more smaller crowdfunding firms will focus on some vertical sub-fields, such as used cars, agricultural products, catering, and film and television, to become a "small but valued" platform with higher success rate. Specialization and refinement will become a trend of crowdfunding development in the near future.

8.4 Becoming Mainstream Via Mobile Phones

Crowdfunding develops rapidly in China in the recent years, but there is still great potential for its further growth with more people's participation, as crowdfunding has not been as widely known in China as its potentials may allow at present. In the future, this situation could be altered by a game changer,—smart mobile phones, which may help elevate the crowdfunding to become the mainstream of financing with smaller scale. Relying on the "anytime and anywhere" mobile interfaces, investors can access to the latest news about crowdfunding and other parts of the financial market around the clock and across different geographical regions via their mobile phones. They can not only better understand the listed projects, but also gain experience in using modern technology to conduct and manage their investment activities. The investors can invest in any listed projects that they are interested by some simple moves of their fingers, anytime and anywhere. This process could be as fast and convenient as booking a Uber car.

8.5 More Transparent Information Disclosure

In the age of information with fast changes in the technology, business, and market, a more transparent operation of crowdfunding would be expected. Relying on more transparent and orderly operated platforms, investors can have better understanding about the listed projects, and, consequently, make better informed decisions, which will help cultivate a calm and rational investment mentality for smaller investors. For the crowdfunding, transparency refers to a number of issues, including, but not limited to, the degree of the details of the presentation of information for the financing projects, the timeliness of the information disclosure, and the profile of other investors. In particular, after the investors transferred their funds in, the crowdfunding platforms need to keep updating the investors about the dynamics and latest developmental progress of the projects that investors invested, and provide practicable operating procedures to allow the investors to conduct an effective post-investment management.

8.6 Innovation

In May 2015, Chinese Premier Li Keqiang visited several companies on the "Entrepreneur Street" (Chuangye Street) of Zhongguancun, Beijing's silicon valley, including 3W Café. 3W Café was established through crowdfunding by several hundreds of investors, with RMB 60,000 investment for each individual, and the investors include some well-known internet, technology and business elites. Crowdfunding, as an innovation in financing, allows the entrepreneurs of the start-ups to obtain funding through the non-traditional financing channels, and revolutionize the ways of consumptions as well. Following 3W Café, a number of crowdfunded stores emerged in multiple cities. It may be worth mentioning that, by crowdfunding the café shop, the reputation of 3W has been greatly and continuously enhanced, which helped the entrepreneurs of 3W obtain a leading position in the field of start-up incubation as well.

As a brand new concept, the crowdfunding was born with many distinctively innovative elements and vitality for its growth. Even though some innovation plans may have defects or failed, or some ideas cannot be implemented due to the conflicts with the existing policies, it is certainly undeniable that many novel and unique thoughts and ideas from these innovative concepts provided the directions of the future development of crowdfunding industry. Today, as the innovations spring up continuously, crowdfunding industry can be expected to grow significantly with the constant innovations as well by breaking through the traditional way of thinking and operation models, and constantly improving customers' consumption experience.

8.7 Crowdfunding Ecologicalization

The development of crowdfunding cannot solely depend upon the growth of each individual platform, instead, it requires the closer collaboration with other parts of the financial industry, fully utilization of the high efficiency of capital market, and establishment of an entire ecology for the crowdfunding industry. In the future, crowdfunding platforms can be expected to build up closer linkage with angel investment funds and venture service providers for being able to provide more effective, more convenient, and one-stop-shopping type of support for these high-quality start-up projects.

In summary, crowdfunding developed rapidly with increased influence and deeper penetration in many subdivided markets in the recent years in China. Its success in the fields such as smart hardware, automobile, film and television, household consumer goods, and music, has reshaped the way of life of millions of consumers nationwide, while the doors of many more promising markets are widely open to its further development. Crowdfunding not only helps increase the consumption and investment—two critical engines of economic growth, but also changes the ways of financing in an innovative way. With the increased government supporting policies and stricter regulations issued at the same time, and the massive entry of business giants such as JD Dongjia, Baidu Baizhong, Antsdaq, 360 Taojin, and Suning Private Equity, the crowdfunding industry in China can be expected to be on track with a more standardized, regulated, and healthier development path for the years to come.

References

1. Z. Liu, K. Wu, Origin, development and prospect of crowdfunding financing. Hainan Finance **6**, 77–81 (2014)
2. Noah Network Star, Analysis on the profiting model of equity crowdfunding platform [R/OL], 2016, http://mt.sohu.com/20160202/n436672131.shtml
3. M. Liu, The age of application of internet on vehicles comes formally. Chin. Qual. Long **1**, 70–71 (2015)
4. C. Yang, The key point of crowdfunding that solves the difficulties of the general public is "return". J. Urban Dev. **7**, 36–37 (2015)
5. G. Du, Five pits in equity crowdfunding investment. Gen. Finan. **9**, 39–41 (2015)
6. Z. Liu, Opportunity or pit depends on "integrity + credit". Gen. Finan. 9, 34–35 (2015)
7. M. Luo, The first year of equity crowdfunding. Gen. Finan. **9**, 32–33 (2015)
8. A. Li, Internet equity financing model and its legal analysis. Gen. Finan. **9**, 79–80 (2015)
9. H. Xie, Under new laws, where is the roundabout space of "equity crowdfunding". Gen. Finan. **9**, 36–38 (2015)
10. Z. Du, Liu Hui, In the age of "exposed" crowdfunding, law life-buoy is necessary. J. Law Life **21**, 19–21 (2015)
11. S. Yu, Analysis on the type of real estate crowdfunding. J. Shanghai Real Estate **03**, 23–24 (2015)
12. D. Yang, L. Su, Operating mode and risk prevention of equity crowdfunding platform. J. Nat. Prosecutors Coll. **4**, 157–168 (2014)
13. J.G. Wang, J. Yang, *Financing Without Bank Loans—New Alternatives for Funding SMEs in China* (Springer, Berlin, 2016)
14. J.G. Wang, H. Xu, *Financing the Underfinanced—Online Lending in China* (Springer, Berlin, 2015)
15. J.G. Wang, J. Yang, *Who Gets Funds from China's Capital Market?—A Micro View of China's Economy via Case Studies on Listed Chinese SMEs* (Springer, Berlin, 2014)

J.G. Wang et al. (eds.), *Financing from Masses*,
https://doi.org/10.1007/978-981-10-5843-1

H.-Y. Wang et al. (eds.), *Biorefining from Microa*
https://doi.org/10.1007/978-981-10-5842-

MIX
Papier aus verantwortungsvollen Quellen
Paper from responsible sources
FSC® C105338

If you have any concerns about our products,
you can contact us on
ProductSafety@springernature.com

In case Publisher is established outside the EU,
the EU authorized representative is:
Springer Nature Customer Service Center GmbH
Europaplatz 3, 69115 Heidelberg, Germany

Printed by Libri Plureos GmbH
in Hamburg, Germany